THE DREAM JOURNAL

Name: _____

Phone: _____

E-mail: _____

···✿···

Date: _____ ☐ ☐ ☐ ☐ ☐ ☐ ☐
Sun Mon Tue Wed Thur Fri Sat

Feelings before sleep: _____

Quality of sleep: ☐ Good ☐ Medium ☐ Bad

Type of dream: ☐ Lucid ☐ Nightmare
☐ Positive ☐ Other: _____

Have you had these dreams before?

☐ Yes ☐ No
☐ Multiple ☐ I don't know

Dream description: _____
_____
_____
_____
_____
_____
_____
_____

Dream interpretation: _____
_____
_____
_____
_____

···✿···

Time period of the dream: ☐ Past ☐ Present

☐ Future ☐ Unknown

Feelings present in the dream:

☐ Fear ☐ Anger ☐ Freedom ☐ Paralysis

☐ Happiness ☐ Sadness ☐ Panic ☐ Love

☐ Doubt ☐ Boredom ☐ Peace ☐ Vulnerability

☐ Luck ☐ Guilt ☐ Horror ☐ Disappointment

☐ Other: _____

The dream featured:

Symbols	Things	Colors	People	Places

Themes	☐ Home	☐ Weather	☐ Fire
☐ Other:	☐ Family	☐ Earth	☐ Water
_____	☐ Childhood	☐ Space	☐ Money
_____	☐ Animals	☐ Vehicles	☐ Health
_____	☐ Friends	☐ Supernatural	☐ Hobbies
_____	☐ Relatives	☐ Technology	☐ Music
	☐ Traveling	☐ Nakedness	☐ Work

···�֍···

Date: _____ ☐   ☐   ☐   ☐   ☐   ☐   ☐
                       Sun   Mon   Tue   Wed   Thur   Fri   Sat

Feelings before sleep: _____

Quality of sleep: ☐ Good   ☐ Medium   ☐ Bad

Type of dream: ☐ Lucid   ☐ Nightmare
                   ☐ Positive   ☐ Other: _____

Have you had these dreams before?

              ☐ Yes   ☐ No
              ☐ Multiple   ☐ I don't know

Dream description: _____
_____
_____
_____
_____
_____
_____
_____

Dream interpretation:_____
_____
_____
_____
_____

···✖···

Time period of the dream: ☐ Past ☐ Present

☐ Future ☐ Unknown

Feelings present in the dream:

☐ Fear ☐ Anger ☐ Freedom ☐ Paralysis

☐ Happiness ☐ Sadness ☐ Panic ☐ Love

☐ Doubt ☐ Boredom ☐ Peace ☐ Vulnerability

☐ Luck ☐ Guilt ☐ Horror ☐ Disappointment

☐ Other: _____

The dream featured:

Symbols	Things	Colors	People	Places

Themes			
☐ Other:	☐ Home	☐ Weather	☐ Fire
_____	☐ Family	☐ Earth	☐ Water
_____	☐ Childhood	☐ Space	☐ Money
_____	☐ Animals	☐ Vehicles	☐ Health
_____	☐ Friends	☐ Supernatural	☐ Hobbies
_____	☐ Relatives	☐ Technology	☐ Music
	☐ Traveling	☐ Nakedness	☐ Work

Date: _____ ☐ ☐ ☐ ☐ ☐ ☐ ☐
                                  Sun Mon Tue Wed Thur Fri Sat

Feelings before sleep: _____

Quality of sleep: ☐ Good   ☐ Medium ☐ Bad

Type of dream: ☐ Lucid   ☐ Nightmare
                      ☐ Positive   ☐ Other: _____

Have you had these dreams before?

        ☐ Yes   ☐ No
        ☐ Multiple ☐ I don't know

Dream description: _____
_____
_____
_____
_____
_____
_____
_____

Dream interpretation: _____
_____
_____
_____
_____

Time period of the dream: ☐ Past ☐ Present

☐ Future ☐ Unknown

Feelings present in the dream:

☐ Fear	☐ Anger	☐ Freedom	☐ Paralysis
☐ Happiness	☐ Sadness	☐ Panic	☐ Love
☐ Doubt	☐ Boredom	☐ Peace	☐ Vulnerability
☐ Luck	☐ Guilt	☐ Horror	☐ Disappointment

☐ Other: _____

The dream featured:

Symbols	Things	Colors	People	Places

Themes	☐ Home	☐ Weather	☐ Fire
☐ Other:	☐ Family	☐ Earth	☐ Water
_____	☐ Childhood	☐ Space	☐ Money
_____	☐ Animals	☐ Vehicles	☐ Health
_____	☐ Friends	☐ Supernatural	☐ Hobbies
_____	☐ Relatives	☐ Technology	☐ Music
	☐ Traveling	☐ Nakedness	☐ Work

···�֎···

Date: _____ ☐ ☐ ☐ ☐ ☐ ☐ ☐
                       Sun Mon Tue Wed Thur Fri Sat

Feelings before sleep: _____

Quality of sleep: ☐ Good   ☐ Medium   ☐ Bad

Type of dream: ☐ Lucid   ☐ Nightmare
                      ☐ Positive ☐ Other: _____

Have you had these dreams before?

                      ☐ Yes   ☐ No
                      ☐ Multiple ☐ I don't know

Dream description: _____
_____
_____
_____
_____
_____
_____

Dream interpretation:_____
_____
_____
_____
_____

···✖···

···✤···

Time period of the dream: ☐ Past   ☐ Present

☐ Future   ☐ Unknown

Feelings present in the dream:

☐ Fear   ☐ Anger   ☐ Freedom   ☐ Paralysis

☐ Happiness   ☐ Sadness   ☐ Panic   ☐ Love

☐ Doubt   ☐ Boredom   ☐ Peace   ☐ Vulnerability

☐ Luck   ☐ Guilt   ☐ Horror   ☐ Disappointment

☐ Other: _____

The dream featured:

Symbols	Things	Colors	People	Places

Themes			
☐ Other:	☐ Home	☐ Weather	☐ Fire
_____	☐ Family	☐ Earth	☐ Water
_____	☐ Childhood	☐ Space	☐ Money
_____	☐ Animals	☐ Vehicles	☐ Health
_____	☐ Friends	☐ Supernatural	☐ Hobbies
_____	☐ Relatives	☐ Technology	☐ Music
	☐ Traveling	☐ Nakedness	☐ Work

···✤···

···�֍···

Date: _____ ☐ ☐ ☐ ☐ ☐ ☐ ☐
Sun Mon Tue Wed Thur Fri Sat

Feelings before sleep: _____

Quality of sleep: ☐ Good ☐ Medium ☐ Bad

Type of dream: ☐ Lucid ☐ Nightmare
☐ Positive ☐ Other: _____

Have you had these dreams before?

☐ Yes ☐ No
☐ Multiple ☐ I don't know

Dream description: _____
_____
_____
_____
_____
_____
_____
_____

Dream interpretation:_____
_____
_____
_____
_____

···✖···

Time period of the dream: ☐ Past   ☐ Present

☐ Future   ☐ Unknown

Feelings present in the dream:

☐ Fear   ☐ Anger   ☐ Freedom   ☐ Paralysis

☐ Happiness   ☐ Sadness   ☐ Panic   ☐ Love

☐ Doubt   ☐ Boredom   ☐ Peace   ☐ Vulnerability

☐ Luck   ☐ Guilt   ☐ Horror   ☐ Disappointment

☐ Other: _____

The dream featured:

Symbols	Things	Colors	People	Places

Themes	☐ Home	☐ Weather	☐ Fire
☐ Other:	☐ Family	☐ Earth	☐ Water
_____	☐ Childhood	☐ Space	☐ Money
_____	☐ Animals	☐ Vehicles	☐ Health
_____	☐ Friends	☐ Supernatural	☐ Hobbies
_____	☐ Relatives	☐ Technology	☐ Music
	☐ Traveling	☐ Nakedness	☐ Work

Date: _____ ☐ ☐ ☐ ☐ ☐ ☐ ☐
                      Sun Mon Tue Wed Thur Fri Sat

Feelings before sleep: _____

Quality of sleep: ☐ Good   ☐ Medium ☐ Bad

Type of dream: ☐ Lucid   ☐ Nightmare
                      ☐ Positive ☐ Other: _____

Have you had these dreams before?

                      ☐ Yes   ☐ No
                      ☐ Multiple ☐ I don't know

Dream description: _____
_____
_____
_____
_____
_____
_____
_____

Dream interpretation:_____
_____
_____
_____
_____

Time period of the dream:
☐ Past ☐ Present
☐ Future ☐ Unknown

Feelings present in the dream:

☐ Fear ☐ Anger ☐ Freedom ☐ Paralysis

☐ Happiness ☐ Sadness ☐ Panic ☐ Love

☐ Doubt ☐ Boredom ☐ Peace ☐ Vulnerability

☐ Luck ☐ Guilt ☐ Horror ☐ Disappointment

☐ Other: _____

The dream featured:

Symbols	Things	Colors	People	Places

Themes			
☐ Other:	☐ Home	☐ Weather	☐ Fire
_____	☐ Family	☐ Earth	☐ Water
_____	☐ Childhood	☐ Space	☐ Money
_____	☐ Animals	☐ Vehicles	☐ Health
_____	☐ Friends	☐ Supernatural	☐ Hobbies
_____	☐ Relatives	☐ Technology	☐ Music
	☐ Traveling	☐ Nakedness	☐ Work

···❈···

Date: _____ ☐ ☐ ☐ ☐ ☐ ☐ ☐
Sun Mon Tue Wed Thur Fri Sat

Feelings before sleep: _____

Quality of sleep: ☐ Good ☐ Medium ☐ Bad

Type of dream: ☐ Lucid ☐ Nightmare
☐ Positive ☐ Other: _____

Have you had these dreams before?

☐ Yes ☐ No
☐ Multiple ☐ I don't know

Dream description: _____
_____
_____
_____
_____
_____
_____

Dream interpretation:_____
_____
_____
_____
_____

···❈···

Time period of the dream: ☐ Past   ☐ Present

☐ Future   ☐ Unknown

Feelings present in the dream:

☐ Fear   ☐ Anger   ☐ Freedom   ☐ Paralysis

☐ Happiness   ☐ Sadness   ☐ Panic   ☐ Love

☐ Doubt   ☐ Boredom   ☐ Peace   ☐ Vulnerability

☐ Luck   ☐ Guilt   ☐ Horror   ☐ Disappointment

☐ Other: _____

The dream featured:

Symbols	Things	Colors	People	Places

Themes	☐ Home	☐ Weather	☐ Fire
☐ Other:	☐ Family	☐ Earth	☐ Water
_____	☐ Childhood	☐ Space	☐ Money
_____	☐ Animals	☐ Vehicles	☐ Health
_____	☐ Friends	☐ Supernatural	☐ Hobbies
_____	☐ Relatives	☐ Technology	☐ Music
	☐ Traveling	☐ Nakedness	☐ Work

Date: ____________ ☐ Sun ☐ Mon ☐ Tue ☐ Wed ☐ Thur ☐ Fri ☐ Sat

Feelings before sleep: ____________________________________

Quality of sleep: ☐ Good ☐ Medium ☐ Bad

Type of dream: ☐ Lucid ☐ Nightmare

☐ Positive ☐ Other: ____________

Have you had these dreams before?

☐ Yes ☐ No

☐ Multiple ☐ I don't know

Dream description: ____________________________________

Dream interpretation: ____________________________________

Time period of the dream: ☐ Past ☐ Present

☐ Future ☐ Unknown

Feelings present in the dream:

☐ Fear ☐ Anger ☐ Freedom ☐ Paralysis

☐ Happiness ☐ Sadness ☐ Panic ☐ Love

☐ Doubt ☐ Boredom ☐ Peace ☐ Vulnerability

☐ Luck ☐ Guilt ☐ Horror ☐ Disappointment

☐ Other: _____

The dream featured:

Symbols	Things	Colors	People	Places

Themes	☐ Home	☐ Weather	☐ Fire
☐ Other:	☐ Family	☐ Earth	☐ Water
_____	☐ Childhood	☐ Space	☐ Money
_____	☐ Animals	☐ Vehicles	☐ Health
_____	☐ Friends	☐ Supernatural	☐ Hobbies
_____	☐ Relatives	☐ Technology	☐ Music
	☐ Traveling	☐ Nakedness	☐ Work

···✤···

Date: _____ ☐ ☐ ☐ ☐ ☐ ☐ ☐
Sun Mon Tue Wed Thur Fri Sat

Feelings before sleep: _____

Quality of sleep: ☐ Good ☐ Medium ☐ Bad

Type of dream: ☐ Lucid ☐ Nightmare
               ☐ Positive ☐ Other: _____

Have you had these dreams before?

☐ Yes ☐ No
☐ Multiple ☐ I don't know

Dream description: _____
_____
_____
_____
_____
_____
_____
_____

Dream interpretation: _____
_____
_____
_____
_____

···✤···

Time period of the dream: ☐ Past   ☐ Present

                            ☐ Future   ☐ Unknown

Feelings present in the dream:

☐ Fear   ☐ Anger   ☐ Freedom   ☐ Paralysis

☐ Happiness   ☐ Sadness   ☐ Panic   ☐ Love

☐ Doubt   ☐ Boredom   ☐ Peace   ☐ Vulnerability

☐ Luck   ☐ Guilt   ☐ Horror   ☐ Disappointment

☐ Other: _____

The dream featured:

Symbols	Things	Colors	People	Places

Themes			
☐ Other:	☐ Home	☐ Weather	☐ Fire
_____	☐ Family	☐ Earth	☐ Water
_____	☐ Childhood	☐ Space	☐ Money
_____	☐ Animals	☐ Vehicles	☐ Health
_____	☐ Friends	☐ Supernatural	☐ Hobbies
	☐ Relatives	☐ Technology	☐ Music
	☐ Traveling	☐ Nakedness	☐ Work

Date: _____ ☐ ☐ ☐ ☐ ☐ ☐ ☐
Sun Mon Tue Wed Thur Fri Sat

Feelings before sleep: _____

Quality of sleep: ☐ Good ☐ Medium ☐ Bad

Type of dream: ☐ Lucid ☐ Nightmare
☐ Positive ☐ Other: _____

Have you had these dreams before?

☐ Yes ☐ No
☐ Multiple ☐ I don't know

Dream description: _____
_____
_____
_____
_____
_____
_____

Dream interpretation:_____
_____
_____
_____
_____

Time period of the dream: ☐ Past ☐ Present

☐ Future ☐ Unknown

Feelings present in the dream:

☐ Fear   ☐ Anger   ☐ Freedom   ☐ Paralysis

☐ Happiness   ☐ Sadness   ☐ Panic   ☐ Love

☐ Doubt   ☐ Boredom   ☐ Peace   ☐ Vulnerability

☐ Luck   ☐ Guilt   ☐ Horror   ☐ Disappointment

☐ Other: _____

The dream featured:

Symbols	Things	Colors	People	Places

Themes	☐ Home	☐ Weather	☐ Fire
☐ Other:	☐ Family	☐ Earth	☐ Water
_____	☐ Childhood	☐ Space	☐ Money
_____	☐ Animals	☐ Vehicles	☐ Health
_____	☐ Friends	☐ Supernatural	☐ Hobbies
_____	☐ Relatives	☐ Technology	☐ Music
	☐ Traveling	☐ Nakedness	☐ Work

···❀···

Date: _____ ☐ ☐ ☐ ☐ ☐ ☐ ☐
                          Sun Mon Tue Wed Thur Fri Sat

Feelings before sleep: _____

Quality of sleep: ☐ Good ☐ Medium ☐ Bad

Type of dream: ☐ Lucid ☐ Nightmare
                      ☐ Positive ☐ Other: _____

Have you had these dreams before?

☐ Yes ☐ No

☐ Multiple ☐ I don't know

Dream description: _____
_____
_____
_____
_____
_____
_____
_____

Dream interpretation: _____
_____
_____
_____
_____

···❀···

Time period of the dream:
☐ Past   ☐ Present
☐ Future   ☐ Unknown

Feelings present in the dream:

☐ Fear   ☐ Anger   ☐ Freedom   ☐ Paralysis

☐ Happiness   ☐ Sadness   ☐ Panic   ☐ Love

☐ Doubt   ☐ Boredom   ☐ Peace   ☐ Vulnerability

☐ Luck   ☐ Guilt   ☐ Horror   ☐ Disappointment

☐ Other: _____

The dream featured:

Symbols	Things	Colors	People	Places

Themes			
☐ Other:	☐ Home	☐ Weather	☐ Fire
_____	☐ Family	☐ Earth	☐ Water
_____	☐ Childhood	☐ Space	☐ Money
_____	☐ Animals	☐ Vehicles	☐ Health
_____	☐ Friends	☐ Supernatural	☐ Hobbies
	☐ Relatives	☐ Technology	☐ Music
	☐ Traveling	☐ Nakedness	☐ Work

···✿···

Date: _____ ☐ ☐ ☐ ☐ ☐ ☐ ☐
Sun Mon Tue Wed Thur Fri Sat

Feelings before sleep: _____

Quality of sleep: ☐ Good ☐ Medium ☐ Bad

Type of dream: ☐ Lucid ☐ Nightmare
☐ Positive ☐ Other: _____

Have you had these dreams before?

☐ Yes ☐ No
☐ Multiple ☐ I don't know

Dream description: _____
_____
_____
_____
_____
_____
_____
_____

Dream interpretation:_____
_____
_____
_____
_____

···✿···

Time period of the dream: ☐ Past   ☐ Present

                                        ☐ Future   ☐ Unknown

Feelings present in the dream:

☐ Fear   ☐ Anger   ☐ Freedom   ☐ Paralysis

☐ Happiness   ☐ Sadness   ☐ Panic   ☐ Love

☐ Doubt   ☐ Boredom   ☐ Peace   ☐ Vulnerability

☐ Luck   ☐ Guilt   ☐ Horror   ☐ Disappointment

☐ Other: _____

The dream featured:

Symbols	Things	Colors	People	Places

Themes	☐ Home	☐ Weather	☐ Fire
☐ Other:	☐ Family	☐ Earth	☐ Water
_____	☐ Childhood	☐ Space	☐ Money
_____	☐ Animals	☐ Vehicles	☐ Health
_____	☐ Friends	☐ Supernatural	☐ Hobbies
_____	☐ Relatives	☐ Technology	☐ Music
	☐ Traveling	☐ Nakedness	☐ Work

Date: _____ ☐   ☐   ☐   ☐   ☐   ☐   ☐
                             Sun   Mon   Tue   Wed   Thur   Fri   Sat

Feelings before sleep: _____

Quality of sleep: ☐ Good   ☐ Medium   ☐ Bad

Type of dream: ☐ Lucid   ☐ Nightmare
                      ☐ Positive   ☐ Other: _____

Have you had these dreams before?

              ☐ Yes   ☐ No

              ☐ Multiple   ☐ I don't know

Dream description: _____
_____
_____
_____
_____
_____
_____
_____

Dream interpretation: _____
_____
_____
_____
_____

Time period of the dream: ☐ Past ☐ Present ☐ Future ☐ Unknown

Feelings present in the dream:

☐ Fear	☐ Anger	☐ Freedom	☐ Paralysis
☐ Happiness	☐ Sadness	☐ Panic	☐ Love
☐ Doubt	☐ Boredom	☐ Peace	☐ Vulnerability
☐ Luck	☐ Guilt	☐ Horror	☐ Disappointment

☐ Other: ______________________________

The dream featured:

Symbols	Things	Colors	People	Places
Themes	☐ Home	☐ Weather	☐ Fire	
☐ Other:	☐ Family	☐ Earth	☐ Water	
________	☐ Childhood	☐ Space	☐ Money	
________	☐ Animals	☐ Vehicles	☐ Health	
________	☐ Friends	☐ Supernatural	☐ Hobbies	
________	☐ Relatives	☐ Technology	☐ Music	
	☐ Traveling	☐ Nakedness	☐ Work	

Date: _____ ☐ ☐ ☐ ☐ ☐ ☐ ☐
                                      Sun Mon Tue Wed Thur Fri Sat

Feelings before sleep: _____

Quality of sleep: ☐ Good   ☐ Medium ☐ Bad

Type of dream: ☐ Lucid   ☐ Nightmare
                         ☐ Positive ☐ Other: _____

Have you had these dreams before?

        ☐ Yes   ☐ No
        ☐ Multiple ☐ I don't know

Dream description: _____
_____
_____
_____
_____
_____
_____
_____

Dream interpretation: _____
_____
_____
_____
_____

Time period of the dream: ☐ Past   ☐ Present

☐ Future   ☐ Unknown

Feelings present in the dream:

☐ Fear   ☐ Anger   ☐ Freedom   ☐ Paralysis

☐ Happiness   ☐ Sadness   ☐ Panic   ☐ Love

☐ Doubt   ☐ Boredom   ☐ Peace   ☐ Vulnerability

☐ Luck   ☐ Guilt   ☐ Horror   ☐ Disappointment

☐ Other: _____

The dream featured:

Symbols	Things	Colors	People	Places

Themes			
☐ Other:	☐ Home	☐ Weather	☐ Fire
_____	☐ Family	☐ Earth	☐ Water
_____	☐ Childhood	☐ Space	☐ Money
_____	☐ Animals	☐ Vehicles	☐ Health
_____	☐ Friends	☐ Supernatural	☐ Hobbies
_____	☐ Relatives	☐ Technology	☐ Music
	☐ Traveling	☐ Nakedness	☐ Work

···❀···

Date: _____ ☐   ☐   ☐   ☐   ☐   ☐   ☐
                                Sun   Mon   Tue   Wed   Thur   Fri   Sat

Feelings before sleep: _____

Quality of sleep: ☐ Good   ☐ Medium   ☐ Bad

Type of dream: ☐ Lucid   ☐ Nightmare
                     ☐ Positive   ☐ Other: _____

Have you had these dreams before?

           ☐ Yes   ☐ No
           ☐ Multiple ☐ I don't know

Dream description: _____

_____

_____

_____

_____

_____

_____

_____

Dream interpretation: _____

_____

_____

_____

_____

···❀···

Time period of the dream: ☐ Past   ☐ Present

☐ Future   ☐ Unknown

Feelings present in the dream:

☐ Fear   ☐ Anger   ☐ Freedom   ☐ Paralysis

☐ Happiness   ☐ Sadness   ☐ Panic   ☐ Love

☐ Doubt   ☐ Boredom   ☐ Peace   ☐ Vulnerability

☐ Luck   ☐ Guilt   ☐ Horror   ☐ Disappointment

☐ Other: _____

The dream featured:

Symbols	Things	Colors	People	Places

Themes			
☐ Other:	☐ Home	☐ Weather	☐ Fire
_____	☐ Family	☐ Earth	☐ Water
_____	☐ Childhood	☐ Space	☐ Money
_____	☐ Animals	☐ Vehicles	☐ Health
_____	☐ Friends	☐ Supernatural	☐ Hobbies
_____	☐ Relatives	☐ Technology	☐ Music
	☐ Traveling	☐ Nakedness	☐ Work

Date: _____ ☐ ☐ ☐ ☐ ☐ ☐ ☐
                        Sun Mon Tue Wed Thur Fri Sat

Feelings before sleep: _____

Quality of sleep: ☐ Good   ☐ Medium   ☐ Bad

Type of dream: ☐ Lucid   ☐ Nightmare
                     ☐ Positive ☐ Other: _____

Have you had these dreams before?

                     ☐ Yes   ☐ No
                     ☐ Multiple ☐ I don't know

Dream description: _____
_____
_____
_____
_____
_____
_____

Dream interpretation: _____
_____
_____
_____
_____

Time period of the dream: ☐ Past   ☐ Present

☐ Future   ☐ Unknown

Feelings present in the dream:

☐ Fear   ☐ Anger   ☐ Freedom   ☐ Paralysis

☐ Happiness   ☐ Sadness   ☐ Panic   ☐ Love

☐ Doubt   ☐ Boredom   ☐ Peace   ☐ Vulnerability

☐ Luck   ☐ Guilt   ☐ Horror   ☐ Disappointment

☐ Other: _____

The dream featured:

Symbols	Things	Colors	People	Places

Themes	☐ Home	☐ Weather	☐ Fire
☐ Other:	☐ Family	☐ Earth	☐ Water
_____	☐ Childhood	☐ Space	☐ Money
_____	☐ Animals	☐ Vehicles	☐ Health
_____	☐ Friends	☐ Supernatural	☐ Hobbies
_____	☐ Relatives	☐ Technology	☐ Music
	☐ Traveling	☐ Nakedness	☐ Work

Date: _____ ☐ ☐ ☐ ☐ ☐ ☐ ☐
                        Sun Mon Tue Wed Thur Fri Sat

Feelings before sleep: _____

Quality of sleep: ☐ Good   ☐ Medium   ☐ Bad

Type of dream: ☐ Lucid   ☐ Nightmare
                      ☐ Positive   ☐ Other: _____

Have you had these dreams before?

                      ☐ Yes   ☐ No
                      ☐ Multiple ☐ I don't know

Dream description: _____
_____
_____
_____
_____
_____
_____
_____

Dream interpretation:_____
_____
_____
_____
_____

Time period of the dream: ☐ Past   ☐ Present

☐ Future   ☐ Unknown

Feelings present in the dream:

☐ Fear   ☐ Anger   ☐ Freedom   ☐ Paralysis

☐ Happiness   ☐ Sadness   ☐ Panic   ☐ Love

☐ Doubt   ☐ Boredom   ☐ Peace   ☐ Vulnerability

☐ Luck   ☐ Guilt   ☐ Horror   ☐ Disappointment

☐ Other: _____

The dream featured:

Symbols	Things	Colors	People	Places

Themes	☐ Home	☐ Weather	☐ Fire
☐ Other:	☐ Family	☐ Earth	☐ Water
_____	☐ Childhood	☐ Space	☐ Money
_____	☐ Animals	☐ Vehicles	☐ Health
_____	☐ Friends	☐ Supernatural	☐ Hobbies
_____	☐ Relatives	☐ Technology	☐ Music
	☐ Traveling	☐ Nakedness	☐ Work

···�֎···

Date: _____ ☐ ☐ ☐ ☐ ☐ ☐ ☐
　　　　　　　　　　　 Sun　Mon　Tue　Wed　Thur　Fri　Sat

Feelings before sleep: _____

Quality of sleep:　　☐ Good　　☐ Medium　☐ Bad

Type of dream:　　　☐ Lucid　　☐ Nightmare
　　　　　　　　　　☐ Positive　☐ Other: _____

Have you had these dreams before?

　　　　　　　　　☐ Yes　　☐ No
　　　　　　　　　☐ Multiple　☐ I don't know

Dream description: _____
_____
_____
_____
_____
_____
_____

Dream interpretation:_____
_____
_____
_____
_____

···✖···

Time period of the dream: ☐ Past ☐ Present

☐ Future ☐ Unknown

Feelings present in the dream:

☐ Fear ☐ Anger ☐ Freedom ☐ Paralysis

☐ Happiness ☐ Sadness ☐ Panic ☐ Love

☐ Doubt ☐ Boredom ☐ Peace ☐ Vulnerability

☐ Luck ☐ Guilt ☐ Horror ☐ Disappointment

☐ Other: _____

The dream featured:

Symbols	Things	Colors	People	Places

Themes	☐ Home	☐ Weather	☐ Fire
☐ Other:	☐ Family	☐ Earth	☐ Water
_____	☐ Childhood	☐ Space	☐ Money
_____	☐ Animals	☐ Vehicles	☐ Health
_____	☐ Friends	☐ Supernatural	☐ Hobbies
_____	☐ Relatives	☐ Technology	☐ Music
	☐ Traveling	☐ Nakedness	☐ Work

Date: _____ ☐ ☐ ☐ ☐ ☐ ☐ ☐
                     Sun Mon Tue Wed Thur Fri Sat

Feelings before sleep: _____

Quality of sleep: ☐ Good   ☐ Medium   ☐ Bad

Type of dream: ☐ Lucid   ☐ Nightmare
                     ☐ Positive ☐ Other: _____

Have you had these dreams before?

                     ☐ Yes   ☐ No
                     ☐ Multiple ☐ I don't know

Dream description: _____
_____
_____
_____
_____
_____
_____
_____

Dream interpretation: _____
_____
_____
_____
_____

Time period of the dream: ☐ Past   ☐ Present

☐ Future   ☐ Unknown

Feelings present in the dream:

☐ Fear   ☐ Anger   ☐ Freedom   ☐ Paralysis

☐ Happiness   ☐ Sadness   ☐ Panic   ☐ Love

☐ Doubt   ☐ Boredom   ☐ Peace   ☐ Vulnerability

☐ Luck   ☐ Guilt   ☐ Horror   ☐ Disappointment

☐ Other: _____

The dream featured:

Symbols	Things	Colors	People	Places

Themes	☐ Home	☐ Weather	☐ Fire
☐ Other:	☐ Family	☐ Earth	☐ Water
_____	☐ Childhood	☐ Space	☐ Money
_____	☐ Animals	☐ Vehicles	☐ Health
_____	☐ Friends	☐ Supernatural	☐ Hobbies
_____	☐ Relatives	☐ Technology	☐ Music
	☐ Traveling	☐ Nakedness	☐ Work

···❁···

Date: _____ ☐ ☐ ☐ ☐ ☐ ☐ ☐
Sun Mon Tue Wed Thur Fri Sat

Feelings before sleep: _____

Quality of sleep: ☐ Good ☐ Medium ☐ Bad

Type of dream: ☐ Lucid ☐ Nightmare
☐ Positive ☐ Other: _____

Have you had these dreams before?

☐ Yes ☐ No
☐ Multiple ☐ I don't know

Dream description: _____
_____
_____
_____
_____
_____
_____

Dream interpretation: _____
_____
_____
_____
_____

···❁···

Time period of the dream: ☐ Past   ☐ Present

☐ Future   ☐ Unknown

Feelings present in the dream:

☐ Fear   ☐ Anger   ☐ Freedom   ☐ Paralysis

☐ Happiness   ☐ Sadness   ☐ Panic   ☐ Love

☐ Doubt   ☐ Boredom   ☐ Peace   ☐ Vulnerability

☐ Luck   ☐ Guilt   ☐ Horror   ☐ Disappointment

☐ Other: _____

The dream featured:

Symbols	Things	Colors	People	Places

Themes			
☐ Other:	☐ Home	☐ Weather	☐ Fire
_____	☐ Family	☐ Earth	☐ Water
_____	☐ Childhood	☐ Space	☐ Money
_____	☐ Animals	☐ Vehicles	☐ Health
_____	☐ Friends	☐ Supernatural	☐ Hobbies
	☐ Relatives	☐ Technology	☐ Music
	☐ Traveling	☐ Nakedness	☐ Work

···❄···

Date: _____ ☐   ☐   ☐   ☐   ☐   ☐   ☐

                                  Sun   Mon   Tue   Wed   Thur   Fri   Sat

Feelings before sleep: _____

Quality of sleep: ☐ Good   ☐ Medium   ☐ Bad

Type of dream: ☐ Lucid   ☐ Nightmare

                        ☐ Positive   ☐ Other: _____

Have you had these dreams before?

                 ☐ Yes   ☐ No

                 ☐ Multiple   ☐ I don't know

Dream description: _____

_____

_____

_____

_____

_____

_____

_____

Dream interpretation:_____

_____

_____

_____

_____

···❄···

Time period of the dream: ☐ Past ☐ Present

☐ Future ☐ Unknown

Feelings present in the dream:

☐ Fear ☐ Anger ☐ Freedom ☐ Paralysis

☐ Happiness ☐ Sadness ☐ Panic ☐ Love

☐ Doubt ☐ Boredom ☐ Peace ☐ Vulnerability

☐ Luck ☐ Guilt ☐ Horror ☐ Disappointment

☐ Other: _____

The dream featured:

Symbols	Things	Colors	People	Places

Themes	☐ Home	☐ Weather	☐ Fire
☐ Other:	☐ Family	☐ Earth	☐ Water
_____	☐ Childhood	☐ Space	☐ Money
_____	☐ Animals	☐ Vehicles	☐ Health
_____	☐ Friends	☐ Supernatural	☐ Hobbies
_____	☐ Relatives	☐ Technology	☐ Music
	☐ Traveling	☐ Nakedness	☐ Work

···❈···

Date: _____ ☐ ☐ ☐ ☐ ☐ ☐ ☐
                      Sun Mon Tue Wed Thur Fri Sat

Feelings before sleep: _____

Quality of sleep: ☐ Good   ☐ Medium   ☐ Bad

Type of dream: ☐ Lucid   ☐ Nightmare
                      ☐ Positive   ☐ Other: _____

Have you had these dreams before?

                      ☐ Yes   ☐ No
                      ☐ Multiple ☐ I don't know

Dream description: _____
_____
_____
_____
_____
_____
_____

Dream interpretation: _____
_____
_____
_____
_____

···❈···

···❋···

Time period of the dream: ☐ Past   ☐ Present

☐ Future   ☐ Unknown

Feelings present in the dream:

☐ Fear   ☐ Anger   ☐ Freedom   ☐ Paralysis

☐ Happiness ☐ Sadness   ☐ Panic   ☐ Love

☐ Doubt   ☐ Boredom   ☐ Peace   ☐ Vulnerability

☐ Luck   ☐ Guilt   ☐ Horror   ☐ Disappointment

☐ Other: _____

The dream featured:

Symbols	Things	Colors	People	Places

Themes	☐ Home	☐ Weather	☐ Fire
☐ Other:	☐ Family	☐ Earth	☐ Water
_____	☐ Childhood	☐ Space	☐ Money
_____	☐ Animals	☐ Vehicles	☐ Health
_____	☐ Friends	☐ Supernatural	☐ Hobbies
_____	☐ Relatives	☐ Technology	☐ Music
	☐ Traveling	☐ Nakedness	☐ Work

···❋···

Date: _____ ☐ ☐ ☐ ☐ ☐ ☐ ☐
                      Sun Mon Tue Wed Thur Fri Sat

Feelings before sleep: _____

Quality of sleep: ☐ Good   ☐ Medium   ☐ Bad

Type of dream: ☐ Lucid   ☐ Nightmare
                       ☐ Positive   ☐ Other: _____

Have you had these dreams before?

                       ☐ Yes   ☐ No
                       ☐ Multiple ☐ I don't know

Dream description: _____
_____
_____
_____
_____
_____
_____

Dream interpretation:_____
_____
_____
_____
_____

Time period of the dream: ☐ Past ☐ Present

☐ Future ☐ Unknown

Feelings present in the dream:

☐ Fear ☐ Anger ☐ Freedom ☐ Paralysis

☐ Happiness ☐ Sadness ☐ Panic ☐ Love

☐ Doubt ☐ Boredom ☐ Peace ☐ Vulnerability

☐ Luck ☐ Guilt ☐ Horror ☐ Disappointment

☐ Other: _____

The dream featured:

Symbols	Things	Colors	People	Places

Themes	☐ Home	☐ Weather	☐ Fire
☐ Other:	☐ Family	☐ Earth	☐ Water
_____	☐ Childhood	☐ Space	☐ Money
_____	☐ Animals	☐ Vehicles	☐ Health
_____	☐ Friends	☐ Supernatural	☐ Hobbies
_____	☐ Relatives	☐ Technology	☐ Music
	☐ Traveling	☐ Nakedness	☐ Work

Date: _____ ☐   ☐   ☐   ☐   ☐   ☐   ☐
                         Sun   Mon   Tue   Wed   Thur   Fri   Sat

Feelings before sleep: _____

Quality of sleep: ☐ Good   ☐ Medium   ☐ Bad

Type of dream: ☐ Lucid   ☐ Nightmare
                       ☐ Positive   ☐ Other: _____

Have you had these dreams before?

                ☐ Yes   ☐ No
                ☐ Multiple   ☐ I don't know

Dream description: _____
_____
_____
_____
_____
_____
_____
_____

Dream interpretation: _____
_____
_____
_____
_____

Time period of the dream: ☐ Past   ☐ Present

☐ Future   ☐ Unknown

Feelings present in the dream:

☐ Fear	☐ Anger	☐ Freedom	☐ Paralysis
☐ Happiness	☐ Sadness	☐ Panic	☐ Love
☐ Doubt	☐ Boredom	☐ Peace	☐ Vulnerability
☐ Luck	☐ Guilt	☐ Horror	☐ Disappointment

☐ Other: _____

The dream featured:

Symbols	Things	Colors	People	Places

Themes	☐ Home	☐ Weather	☐ Fire
☐ Other:	☐ Family	☐ Earth	☐ Water
_____	☐ Childhood	☐ Space	☐ Money
_____	☐ Animals	☐ Vehicles	☐ Health
_____	☐ Friends	☐ Supernatural	☐ Hobbies
_____	☐ Relatives	☐ Technology	☐ Music
	☐ Traveling	☐ Nakedness	☐ Work

Date: _____ ☐ ☐ ☐ ☐ ☐ ☐ ☐
                      Sun Mon Tue Wed Thur Fri Sat

Feelings before sleep: _____

Quality of sleep: ☐ Good   ☐ Medium   ☐ Bad

Type of dream: ☐ Lucid   ☐ Nightmare
                     ☐ Positive ☐ Other: _____

Have you had these dreams before?

                     ☐ Yes   ☐ No
                     ☐ Multiple ☐ I don't know

Dream description: _____
_____
_____
_____
_____
_____
_____

Dream interpretation: _____
_____
_____
_____
_____

Time period of the dream: ☐ Past   ☐ Present

☐ Future ☐ Unknown

Feelings present in the dream:

☐ Fear   ☐ Anger   ☐ Freedom   ☐ Paralysis

☐ Happiness   ☐ Sadness   ☐ Panic   ☐ Love

☐ Doubt   ☐ Boredom   ☐ Peace   ☐ Vulnerability

☐ Luck   ☐ Guilt   ☐ Horror   ☐ Disappointment

☐ Other: _____

The dream featured:

Symbols	Things	Colors	People	Places

Themes			
☐ Other:	☐ Home	☐ Weather	☐ Fire
_____	☐ Family	☐ Earth	☐ Water
_____	☐ Childhood	☐ Space	☐ Money
_____	☐ Animals	☐ Vehicles	☐ Health
_____	☐ Friends	☐ Supernatural	☐ Hobbies
	☐ Relatives	☐ Technology	☐ Music
	☐ Traveling	☐ Nakedness	☐ Work

···❋···

Date: _____ ☐ ☐ ☐ ☐ ☐ ☐ ☐
                          Sun Mon Tue Wed Thur Fri Sat

Feelings before sleep: _____

Quality of sleep: ☐ Good   ☐ Medium ☐ Bad

Type of dream: ☐ Lucid   ☐ Nightmare
                   ☐ Positive ☐ Other: _____

Have you had these dreams before?

    ☐ Yes   ☐ No

    ☐ Multiple ☐ I don't know

Dream description: _____
_____
_____
_____
_____
_____
_____

Dream interpretation:_____
_____
_____
_____
_____

···❋···

Time period of the dream: ☐ Past ☐ Present

☐ Future ☐ Unknown

Feelings present in the dream:

☐ Fear ☐ Anger ☐ Freedom ☐ Paralysis

☐ Happiness ☐ Sadness ☐ Panic ☐ Love

☐ Doubt ☐ Boredom ☐ Peace ☐ Vulnerability

☐ Luck ☐ Guilt ☐ Horror ☐ Disappointment

☐ Other: _____

The dream featured:

Symbols	Things	Colors	People	Places

Themes			
☐ Other:	☐ Home	☐ Weather	☐ Fire
_____	☐ Family	☐ Earth	☐ Water
_____	☐ Childhood	☐ Space	☐ Money
_____	☐ Animals	☐ Vehicles	☐ Health
_____	☐ Friends	☐ Supernatural	☐ Hobbies
_____	☐ Relatives	☐ Technology	☐ Music
	☐ Traveling	☐ Nakedness	☐ Work

··· ❀ ···

Date: _____ ☐ ☐ ☐ ☐ ☐ ☐ ☐
                     Sun Mon Tue Wed Thur Fri Sat

Feelings before sleep: _____

Quality of sleep: ☐ Good   ☐ Medium ☐ Bad

Type of dream: ☐ Lucid   ☐ Nightmare
                     ☐ Positive   ☐ Other: _____

Have you had these dreams before?

                     ☐ Yes   ☐ No
                     ☐ Multiple ☐ I don't know

Dream description: _____
_____
_____
_____
_____
_____
_____
_____

Dream interpretation: _____
_____
_____
_____
_____

··· ❀ ···

Time period of the dream:　　　☐ Past　　　☐ Present

　　　　　　　　　　　　　　　☐ Future　　☐ Unknown

Feelings present in the dream:

☐ Fear　　　☐ Anger　　　☐ Freedom　　☐ Paralysis

☐ Happiness　☐ Sadness　☐ Panic　　　☐ Love

☐ Doubt　　☐ Boredom　☐ Peace　　　☐ Vulnerability

☐ Luck　　　☐ Guilt　　　☐ Horror　　☐ Disappointment

☐ Other: _____

The dream featured:

Symbols	Things	Colors	People	Places

Themes	☐ Home	☐ Weather	☐ Fire
☐ Other:	☐ Family	☐ Earth	☐ Water
_____	☐ Childhood	☐ Space	☐ Money
_____	☐ Animals	☐ Vehicles	☐ Health
_____	☐ Friends	☐ Supernatural	☐ Hobbies
_____	☐ Relatives	☐ Technology	☐ Music
	☐ Traveling	☐ Nakedness	☐ Work

Date: _____ ☐ ☐ ☐ ☐ ☐ ☐ ☐
Sun Mon Tue Wed Thur Fri Sat

Feelings before sleep: _____

Quality of sleep: ☐ Good ☐ Medium ☐ Bad

Type of dream: ☐ Lucid ☐ Nightmare
☐ Positive ☐ Other: _____

Have you had these dreams before?

☐ Yes ☐ No

☐ Multiple ☐ I don't know

Dream description: _____
_____
_____
_____
_____
_____
_____
_____

Dream interpretation: _____
_____
_____
_____
_____

Time period of the dream: ☐ Past   ☐ Present

                           ☐ Future   ☐ Unknown

Feelings present in the dream:

☐ Fear   ☐ Anger   ☐ Freedom   ☐ Paralysis

☐ Happiness   ☐ Sadness   ☐ Panic   ☐ Love

☐ Doubt   ☐ Boredom   ☐ Peace   ☐ Vulnerability

☐ Luck   ☐ Guilt   ☐ Horror   ☐ Disappointment

☐ Other: _____

The dream featured:

Symbols	Things	Colors	People	Places

Themes	☐ Home	☐ Weather	☐ Fire
☐ Other:	☐ Family	☐ Earth	☐ Water
_____	☐ Childhood	☐ Space	☐ Money
_____	☐ Animals	☐ Vehicles	☐ Health
_____	☐ Friends	☐ Supernatural	☐ Hobbies
_____	☐ Relatives	☐ Technology	☐ Music
	☐ Traveling	☐ Nakedness	☐ Work

Date: _____ ☐   ☐   ☐   ☐   ☐   ☐   ☐
                        Sun   Mon   Tue   Wed   Thur   Fri   Sat

Feelings before sleep: _____

Quality of sleep: ☐ Good   ☐ Medium   ☐ Bad

Type of dream: ☐ Lucid   ☐ Nightmare

                    ☐ Positive   ☐ Other: _____

Have you had these dreams before?

           ☐ Yes   ☐ No

           ☐ Multiple   ☐ I don't know

Dream description: _____

_____

_____

_____

_____

_____

_____

Dream interpretation:_____

_____

_____

_____

_____

Time period of the dream:

☐ Past   ☐ Present

☐ Future   ☐ Unknown

Feelings present in the dream:

☐ Fear   ☐ Anger   ☐ Freedom   ☐ Paralysis

☐ Happiness   ☐ Sadness   ☐ Panic   ☐ Love

☐ Doubt   ☐ Boredom   ☐ Peace   ☐ Vulnerability

☐ Luck   ☐ Guilt   ☐ Horror   ☐ Disappointment

☐ Other: _____

The dream featured:

Symbols	Things	Colors	People	Places

Themes			
☐ Other:	☐ Home	☐ Weather	☐ Fire
_____	☐ Family	☐ Earth	☐ Water
_____	☐ Childhood	☐ Space	☐ Money
_____	☐ Animals	☐ Vehicles	☐ Health
_____	☐ Friends	☐ Supernatural	☐ Hobbies
	☐ Relatives	☐ Technology	☐ Music
	☐ Traveling	☐ Nakedness	☐ Work

✻

Date: _____ ☐ ☐ ☐ ☐ ☐ ☐ ☐
                        Sun Mon Tue Wed Thur Fri Sat

Feelings before sleep: _____

Quality of sleep: ☐ Good   ☐ Medium   ☐ Bad

Type of dream: ☐ Lucid   ☐ Nightmare
                     ☐ Positive ☐ Other: _____

Have you had these dreams before?

                ☐ Yes   ☐ No
                ☐ Multiple ☐ I don't know

Dream description: _____
_____
_____
_____
_____
_____
_____
_____

Dream interpretation: _____
_____
_____
_____
_____

✻

Time period of the dream: ☐ Past   ☐ Present

☐ Future   ☐ Unknown

Feelings present in the dream:

☐ Fear   ☐ Anger   ☐ Freedom   ☐ Paralysis

☐ Happiness   ☐ Sadness   ☐ Panic   ☐ Love

☐ Doubt   ☐ Boredom   ☐ Peace   ☐ Vulnerability

☐ Luck   ☐ Guilt   ☐ Horror   ☐ Disappointment

☐ Other: _____

The dream featured:

Symbols	Things	Colors	People	Places

Themes			
☐ Other:	☐ Home	☐ Weather	☐ Fire
_____	☐ Family	☐ Earth	☐ Water
_____	☐ Childhood	☐ Space	☐ Money
_____	☐ Animals	☐ Vehicles	☐ Health
_____	☐ Friends	☐ Supernatural	☐ Hobbies
_____	☐ Relatives	☐ Technology	☐ Music
	☐ Traveling	☐ Nakedness	☐ Work

···❄···

Date: _____ ☐ ☐ ☐ ☐ ☐ ☐ ☐
                      Sun Mon Tue Wed Thur Fri Sat

Feelings before sleep: _____

Quality of sleep: ☐ Good   ☐ Medium   ☐ Bad

Type of dream: ☐ Lucid   ☐ Nightmare
                     ☐ Positive ☐ Other: _____

Have you had these dreams before?

            ☐ Yes   ☐ No
            ☐ Multiple ☐ I don't know

Dream description: _____
_____
_____
_____
_____
_____
_____

Dream interpretation:_____
_____
_____
_____
_____

···❄···

···❁···

Time period of the dream: ☐ Past ☐ Present

☐ Future ☐ Unknown

Feelings present in the dream:

☐ Fear ☐ Anger ☐ Freedom ☐ Paralysis

☐ Happiness ☐ Sadness ☐ Panic ☐ Love

☐ Doubt ☐ Boredom ☐ Peace ☐ Vulnerability

☐ Luck ☐ Guilt ☐ Horror ☐ Disappointment

☐ Other: _____

The dream featured:

Symbols	Things	Colors	People	Places

Themes	☐ Home	☐ Weather	☐ Fire
☐ Other:	☐ Family	☐ Earth	☐ Water
_____	☐ Childhood	☐ Space	☐ Money
_____	☐ Animals	☐ Vehicles	☐ Health
_____	☐ Friends	☐ Supernatural	☐ Hobbies
_____	☐ Relatives	☐ Technology	☐ Music
	☐ Traveling	☐ Nakedness	☐ Work

···❁···

Date: _____ ☐   ☐   ☐   ☐   ☐   ☐   ☐
                           Sun   Mon   Tue   Wed   Thur   Fri   Sat

Feelings before sleep: _____

Quality of sleep: ☐ Good   ☐ Medium   ☐ Bad

Type of dream: ☐ Lucid   ☐ Nightmare
                      ☐ Positive   ☐ Other: _____

Have you had these dreams before?

                   ☐ Yes   ☐ No
                   ☐ Multiple   ☐ I don't know

Dream description: _____
_____
_____
_____
_____
_____
_____
_____

Dream interpretation:_____
_____
_____
_____
_____

Time period of the dream: ☐ Past   ☐ Present
                             ☐ Future   ☐ Unknown

Feelings present in the dream:

☐ Fear   ☐ Anger   ☐ Freedom   ☐ Paralysis

☐ Happiness   ☐ Sadness   ☐ Panic   ☐ Love

☐ Doubt   ☐ Boredom   ☐ Peace   ☐ Vulnerability

☐ Luck   ☐ Guilt   ☐ Horror   ☐ Disappointment

☐ Other: _____

The dream featured:

Symbols	Things	Colors	People	Places

Themes	☐ Home	☐ Weather	☐ Fire
☐ Other:	☐ Family	☐ Earth	☐ Water
_____	☐ Childhood	☐ Space	☐ Money
_____	☐ Animals	☐ Vehicles	☐ Health
_____	☐ Friends	☐ Supernatural	☐ Hobbies
_____	☐ Relatives	☐ Technology	☐ Music
	☐ Traveling	☐ Nakedness	☐ Work

❊

Date: _____ ☐ ☐ ☐ ☐ ☐ ☐ ☐
Sun Mon Tue Wed Thur Fri Sat

Feelings before sleep: _____

Quality of sleep: ☐ Good ☐ Medium ☐ Bad

Type of dream: ☐ Lucid ☐ Nightmare
☐ Positive ☐ Other: _____

Have you had these dreams before?

☐ Yes ☐ No
☐ Multiple ☐ I don't know

Dream description: _____
_____
_____
_____
_____
_____
_____
_____

Dream interpretation:_____
_____
_____
_____
_____

❊

Time period of the dream: ☐ Past   ☐ Present

                           ☐ Future ☐ Unknown

Feelings present in the dream:

☐ Fear   ☐ Anger   ☐ Freedom   ☐ Paralysis

☐ Happiness   ☐ Sadness   ☐ Panic   ☐ Love

☐ Doubt   ☐ Boredom   ☐ Peace   ☐ Vulnerability

☐ Luck   ☐ Guilt   ☐ Horror   ☐ Disappointment

☐ Other: _____

The dream featured:

Symbols	Things	Colors	People	Places

Themes	☐ Home	☐ Weather	☐ Fire
☐ Other:	☐ Family	☐ Earth	☐ Water
_____	☐ Childhood	☐ Space	☐ Money
_____	☐ Animals	☐ Vehicles	☐ Health
_____	☐ Friends	☐ Supernatural	☐ Hobbies
_____	☐ Relatives	☐ Technology	☐ Music
	☐ Traveling	☐ Nakedness	☐ Work

Date: _____ ☐ ☐ ☐ ☐ ☐ ☐ ☐
Sun Mon Tue Wed Thur Fri Sat

Feelings before sleep: _____

Quality of sleep: ☐ Good ☐ Medium ☐ Bad

Type of dream: ☐ Lucid ☐ Nightmare
☐ Positive ☐ Other: _____

Have you had these dreams before?

☐ Yes ☐ No
☐ Multiple ☐ I don't know

Dream description: _____
_____
_____
_____
_____
_____
_____

Dream interpretation: _____
_____
_____
_____
_____

Time period of the dream: ☐ Past   ☐ Present
                           ☐ Future   ☐ Unknown

Feelings present in the dream:

☐ Fear   ☐ Anger   ☐ Freedom   ☐ Paralysis

☐ Happiness   ☐ Sadness   ☐ Panic   ☐ Love

☐ Doubt   ☐ Boredom   ☐ Peace   ☐ Vulnerability

☐ Luck   ☐ Guilt   ☐ Horror   ☐ Disappointment

☐ Other: _____

The dream featured:

Symbols	Things	Colors	People	Places

Themes	☐ Home	☐ Weather	☐ Fire
☐ Other:	☐ Family	☐ Earth	☐ Water
_____	☐ Childhood	☐ Space	☐ Money
_____	☐ Animals	☐ Vehicles	☐ Health
_____	☐ Friends	☐ Supernatural	☐ Hobbies
_____	☐ Relatives	☐ Technology	☐ Music
	☐ Traveling	☐ Nakedness	☐ Work

···✿···

Date: _____ ☐ ☐ ☐ ☐ ☐ ☐ ☐
Sun   Mon   Tue   Wed   Thur   Fri   Sat

Feelings before sleep: _____

Quality of sleep: ☐ Good   ☐ Medium   ☐ Bad

Type of dream: ☐ Lucid   ☐ Nightmare
                 ☐ Positive   ☐ Other: _____

Have you had these dreams before?

☐ Yes   ☐ No
☐ Multiple ☐ I don't know

Dream description: _____
_____
_____
_____
_____
_____
_____

Dream interpretation: _____
_____
_____
_____
_____

···✿···

Time period of the dream: ☐ Past ☐ Present

☐ Future ☐ Unknown

Feelings present in the dream:

☐ Fear ☐ Anger ☐ Freedom ☐ Paralysis

☐ Happiness ☐ Sadness ☐ Panic ☐ Love

☐ Doubt ☐ Boredom ☐ Peace ☐ Vulnerability

☐ Luck ☐ Guilt ☐ Horror ☐ Disappointment

☐ Other: _____

The dream featured:

Symbols	Things	Colors	People	Places

Themes	☐ Home	☐ Weather	☐ Fire
☐ Other:	☐ Family	☐ Earth	☐ Water
_____	☐ Childhood	☐ Space	☐ Money
_____	☐ Animals	☐ Vehicles	☐ Health
_____	☐ Friends	☐ Supernatural	☐ Hobbies
_____	☐ Relatives	☐ Technology	☐ Music
	☐ Traveling	☐ Nakedness	☐ Work

❊

Date: _____ ☐   ☐   ☐   ☐   ☐   ☐   ☐
                  Sun   Mon   Tue   Wed   Thur   Fri   Sat

Feelings before sleep: _____

Quality of sleep: ☐ Good   ☐ Medium   ☐ Bad

Type of dream: ☐ Lucid   ☐ Nightmare
                  ☐ Positive   ☐ Other: _____

Have you had these dreams before?

           ☐ Yes   ☐ No
           ☐ Multiple   ☐ I don't know

Dream description: _____
_____
_____
_____
_____
_____
_____
_____

Dream interpretation:_____
_____
_____
_____
_____

❊

Time period of the dream: ☐ Past ☐ Present

☐ Future ☐ Unknown

Feelings present in the dream:

☐ Fear   ☐ Anger   ☐ Freedom   ☐ Paralysis

☐ Happiness ☐ Sadness ☐ Panic   ☐ Love

☐ Doubt   ☐ Boredom ☐ Peace   ☐ Vulnerability

☐ Luck   ☐ Guilt   ☐ Horror   ☐ Disappointment

☐ Other: _____

The dream featured:

Symbols	Things	Colors	People	Places

Themes	☐ Home	☐ Weather	☐ Fire
☐ Other:	☐ Family	☐ Earth	☐ Water
_____	☐ Childhood	☐ Space	☐ Money
_____	☐ Animals	☐ Vehicles	☐ Health
_____	☐ Friends	☐ Supernatural	☐ Hobbies
_____	☐ Relatives	☐ Technology	☐ Music
	☐ Traveling	☐ Nakedness	☐ Work

❋

Date: _____ ☐   ☐   ☐   ☐   ☐   ☐   ☐
                           Sun   Mon   Tue   Wed   Thur   Fri   Sat

Feelings before sleep: _____

Quality of sleep: ☐ Good   ☐ Medium   ☐ Bad

Type of dream: ☐ Lucid   ☐ Nightmare
                    ☐ Positive   ☐ Other: _____

Have you had these dreams before?

           ☐ Yes   ☐ No

           ☐ Multiple   ☐ I don't know

Dream description: _____

_____

_____

_____

_____

_____

_____

_____

Dream interpretation: _____

_____

_____

_____

_____

❋

Time period of the dream: ☐ Past ☐ Present

☐ Future ☐ Unknown

Feelings present in the dream:

☐ Fear ☐ Anger ☐ Freedom ☐ Paralysis

☐ Happiness ☐ Sadness ☐ Panic ☐ Love

☐ Doubt ☐ Boredom ☐ Peace ☐ Vulnerability

☐ Luck ☐ Guilt ☐ Horror ☐ Disappointment

☐ Other: _____

The dream featured:

Symbols	Things	Colors	People	Places

Themes			
☐ Other:	☐ Home	☐ Weather	☐ Fire
_____	☐ Family	☐ Earth	☐ Water
_____	☐ Childhood	☐ Space	☐ Money
_____	☐ Animals	☐ Vehicles	☐ Health
_____	☐ Friends	☐ Supernatural	☐ Hobbies
	☐ Relatives	☐ Technology	☐ Music
	☐ Traveling	☐ Nakedness	☐ Work

···❋···

Date: _____ ☐ ☐ ☐ ☐ ☐ ☐ ☐
Sun Mon Tue Wed Thur Fri Sat

Feelings before sleep: _____

Quality of sleep: ☐ Good ☐ Medium ☐ Bad

Type of dream: ☐ Lucid ☐ Nightmare
☐ Positive ☐ Other: _____

Have you had these dreams before?

☐ Yes ☐ No
☐ Multiple ☐ I don't know

Dream description: _____
_____
_____
_____
_____
_____
_____
_____

Dream interpretation:_____
_____
_____
_____
_____

···❋···

···❈···

Time period of the dream: ☐ Past   ☐ Present

                             ☐ Future   ☐ Unknown

Feelings present in the dream:

☐ Fear   ☐ Anger   ☐ Freedom   ☐ Paralysis

☐ Happiness   ☐ Sadness   ☐ Panic   ☐ Love

☐ Doubt   ☐ Boredom   ☐ Peace   ☐ Vulnerability

☐ Luck   ☐ Guilt   ☐ Horror   ☐ Disappointment

☐ Other: _____

The dream featured:

Symbols	Things	Colors	People	Places

Themes	☐ Home	☐ Weather	☐ Fire
☐ Other:	☐ Family	☐ Earth	☐ Water
_____	☐ Childhood	☐ Space	☐ Money
_____	☐ Animals	☐ Vehicles	☐ Health
_____	☐ Friends	☐ Supernatural	☐ Hobbies
_____	☐ Relatives	☐ Technology	☐ Music
	☐ Traveling	☐ Nakedness	☐ Work

···❈···

Date: _____ ☐ ☐ ☐ ☐ ☐ ☐ ☐
Sun Mon Tue Wed Thur Fri Sat

Feelings before sleep: _____

Quality of sleep: ☐ Good ☐ Medium ☐ Bad

Type of dream: ☐ Lucid ☐ Nightmare
☐ Positive ☐ Other: _____

Have you had these dreams before?

☐ Yes ☐ No
☐ Multiple ☐ I don't know

Dream description: _____
_____
_____
_____
_____
_____
_____
_____

Dream interpretation:_____
_____
_____
_____
_____

Time period of the dream: ☐ Past ☐ Present

☐ Future ☐ Unknown

Feelings present in the dream:

☐ Fear ☐ Anger ☐ Freedom ☐ Paralysis

☐ Happiness ☐ Sadness ☐ Panic ☐ Love

☐ Doubt ☐ Boredom ☐ Peace ☐ Vulnerability

☐ Luck ☐ Guilt ☐ Horror ☐ Disappointment

☐ Other: _____

The dream featured:

Symbols	Things	Colors	People	Places
Themes	☐ Home	☐ Weather	☐ Fire	
☐ Other:	☐ Family	☐ Earth	☐ Water	
_____	☐ Childhood	☐ Space	☐ Money	
_____	☐ Animals	☐ Vehicles	☐ Health	
_____	☐ Friends	☐ Supernatural	☐ Hobbies	
_____	☐ Relatives	☐ Technology	☐ Music	
	☐ Traveling	☐ Nakedness	☐ Work	

Date: _____ ☐ ☐ ☐ ☐ ☐ ☐ ☐
Sun Mon Tue Wed Thur Fri Sat

Feelings before sleep: _____

Quality of sleep: ☐ Good ☐ Medium ☐ Bad

Type of dream: ☐ Lucid ☐ Nightmare
☐ Positive ☐ Other: _____

Have you had these dreams before?

☐ Yes ☐ No

☐ Multiple ☐ I don't know

Dream description: _____
_____
_____
_____
_____
_____
_____

Dream interpretation:_____
_____
_____
_____
_____

···❁···

Time period of the dream: ☐ Past   ☐ Present

☐ Future   ☐ Unknown

Feelings present in the dream:

☐ Fear   ☐ Anger   ☐ Freedom   ☐ Paralysis

☐ Happiness   ☐ Sadness   ☐ Panic   ☐ Love

☐ Doubt   ☐ Boredom   ☐ Peace   ☐ Vulnerability

☐ Luck   ☐ Guilt   ☐ Horror   ☐ Disappointment

☐ Other: _____

The dream featured:

Symbols	Things	Colors	People	Places

Themes			
☐ Other:	☐ Home	☐ Weather	☐ Fire
_____	☐ Family	☐ Earth	☐ Water
_____	☐ Childhood	☐ Space	☐ Money
_____	☐ Animals	☐ Vehicles	☐ Health
_____	☐ Friends	☐ Supernatural	☐ Hobbies
_____	☐ Relatives	☐ Technology	☐ Music
	☐ Traveling	☐ Nakedness	☐ Work

···❁···

···✳···

Date: _____ ☐ ☐ ☐ ☐ ☐ ☐ ☐
                                    Sun   Mon   Tue Wed Thur Fri Sat

Feelings before sleep: _____

Quality of sleep: ☐ Good   ☐ Medium ☐ Bad

Type of dream: ☐ Lucid   ☐ Nightmare
                      ☐ Positive   ☐ Other: _____

Have you had these dreams before?

     ☐ Yes   ☐ No
     ☐ Multiple ☐ I don't know

Dream description: _____
_____
_____
_____
_____
_____
_____
_____

Dream interpretation:_____
_____
_____
_____
_____

···✳···

Time period of the dream: ☐ Past   ☐ Present

☐ Future   ☐ Unknown

Feelings present in the dream:

☐ Fear   ☐ Anger   ☐ Freedom   ☐ Paralysis

☐ Happiness   ☐ Sadness   ☐ Panic   ☐ Love

☐ Doubt   ☐ Boredom   ☐ Peace   ☐ Vulnerability

☐ Luck   ☐ Guilt   ☐ Horror   ☐ Disappointment

☐ Other: _____

The dream featured:

Symbols	Things	Colors	People	Places

Themes			
☐ Other:	☐ Home	☐ Weather	☐ Fire
_____	☐ Family	☐ Earth	☐ Water
_____	☐ Childhood	☐ Space	☐ Money
_____	☐ Animals	☐ Vehicles	☐ Health
_____	☐ Friends	☐ Supernatural	☐ Hobbies
_____	☐ Relatives	☐ Technology	☐ Music
	☐ Traveling	☐ Nakedness	☐ Work

···❈···

Date: _____ ☐   ☐   ☐   ☐   ☐   ☐   ☐
                            Sun   Mon   Tue   Wed   Thur   Fri   Sat

Feelings before sleep: _____

Quality of sleep: ☐ Good   ☐ Medium   ☐ Bad

Type of dream: ☐ Lucid   ☐ Nightmare
                       ☐ Positive   ☐ Other: _____

Have you had these dreams before?

               ☐ Yes   ☐ No
               ☐ Multiple ☐ I don't know

Dream description: _____

_____

_____

_____

_____

_____

_____

Dream interpretation:_____

_____

_____

_____

_____

···❈···

Time period of the dream: ☐ Past   ☐ Present

☐ Future   ☐ Unknown

Feelings present in the dream:

☐ Fear   ☐ Anger   ☐ Freedom   ☐ Paralysis

☐ Happiness   ☐ Sadness   ☐ Panic   ☐ Love

☐ Doubt   ☐ Boredom   ☐ Peace   ☐ Vulnerability

☐ Luck   ☐ Guilt   ☐ Horror   ☐ Disappointment

☐ Other: _____

The dream featured:

Symbols	Things	Colors	People	Places

Themes	☐ Home	☐ Weather	☐ Fire
☐ Other:	☐ Family	☐ Earth	☐ Water
_____	☐ Childhood	☐ Space	☐ Money
_____	☐ Animals	☐ Vehicles	☐ Health
_____	☐ Friends	☐ Supernatural	☐ Hobbies
_____	☐ Relatives	☐ Technology	☐ Music
	☐ Traveling	☐ Nakedness	☐ Work

···❀···

Date: _____ ☐   ☐   ☐   ☐   ☐   ☐   ☐
                    Sun   Mon   Tue   Wed   Thur   Fri   Sat

Feelings before sleep: _____

Quality of sleep: ☐ Good   ☐ Medium   ☐ Bad

Type of dream: ☐ Lucid   ☐ Nightmare
                   ☐ Positive   ☐ Other: _____

Have you had these dreams before?

           ☐ Yes   ☐ No
           ☐ Multiple ☐ I don't know

Dream description: _____
_____
_____
_____
_____
_____
_____

Dream interpretation: _____
_____
_____
_____
_____

···❀···

Time period of the dream: ☐ Past ☐ Present

☐ Future ☐ Unknown

Feelings present in the dream:

☐ Fear   ☐ Anger   ☐ Freedom   ☐ Paralysis

☐ Happiness ☐ Sadness   ☐ Panic   ☐ Love

☐ Doubt   ☐ Boredom   ☐ Peace   ☐ Vulnerability

☐ Luck   ☐ Guilt   ☐ Horror   ☐ Disappointment

☐ Other: _____

The dream featured:

Symbols	Things	Colors	People	Places

Themes	☐ Home	☐ Weather	☐ Fire
☐ Other:	☐ Family	☐ Earth	☐ Water
_____	☐ Childhood	☐ Space	☐ Money
_____	☐ Animals	☐ Vehicles	☐ Health
_____	☐ Friends	☐ Supernatural	☐ Hobbies
_____	☐ Relatives	☐ Technology	☐ Music
	☐ Traveling	☐ Nakedness	☐ Work

···❊···

Date: _____ ☐ ☐ ☐ ☐ ☐ ☐ ☐
                        Sun Mon Tue Wed Thur Fri Sat

Feelings before sleep: _____

Quality of sleep: ☐ Good   ☐ Medium ☐ Bad

Type of dream: ☐ Lucid   ☐ Nightmare
                     ☐ Positive ☐ Other: _____

Have you had these dreams before?

                     ☐ Yes   ☐ No
                     ☐ Multiple ☐ I don't know

Dream description: _____
_____
_____
_____
_____
_____
_____
_____

Dream interpretation: _____
_____
_____
_____
_____

···❊···

Time period of the dream: ☐ Past ☐ Present

☐ Future ☐ Unknown

Feelings present in the dream:

☐ Fear ☐ Anger ☐ Freedom ☐ Paralysis

☐ Happiness ☐ Sadness ☐ Panic ☐ Love

☐ Doubt ☐ Boredom ☐ Peace ☐ Vulnerability

☐ Luck ☐ Guilt ☐ Horror ☐ Disappointment

☐ Other: _____

The dream featured:

Symbols	Things	Colors	People	Places

Themes	☐ Home	☐ Weather	☐ Fire
☐ Other:	☐ Family	☐ Earth	☐ Water
_____	☐ Childhood	☐ Space	☐ Money
_____	☐ Animals	☐ Vehicles	☐ Health
_____	☐ Friends	☐ Supernatural	☐ Hobbies
_____	☐ Relatives	☐ Technology	☐ Music
	☐ Traveling	☐ Nakedness	☐ Work

···❁···

Date: _____ ☐   ☐   ☐   ☐   ☐   ☐   ☐
                                Sun   Mon   Tue   Wed   Thur   Fri   Sat

Feelings before sleep: _____

Quality of sleep: ☐ Good   ☐ Medium   ☐ Bad

Type of dream: ☐ Lucid   ☐ Nightmare
                      ☐ Positive   ☐ Other: _____

Have you had these dreams before?

             ☐ Yes   ☐ No

             ☐ Multiple   ☐ I don't know

Dream description: _____

_____

_____

_____

_____

_____

_____

Dream interpretation: _____

_____

_____

_____

_____

···❁···

Time period of the dream: ☐ Past ☐ Present

☐ Future ☐ Unknown

Feelings present in the dream:

☐ Fear ☐ Anger ☐ Freedom ☐ Paralysis

☐ Happiness ☐ Sadness ☐ Panic ☐ Love

☐ Doubt ☐ Boredom ☐ Peace ☐ Vulnerability

☐ Luck ☐ Guilt ☐ Horror ☐ Disappointment

☐ Other: _____

The dream featured:

Symbols	Things	Colors	People	Places

Themes	☐ Home	☐ Weather	☐ Fire
☐ Other:	☐ Family	☐ Earth	☐ Water
_____	☐ Childhood	☐ Space	☐ Money
_____	☐ Animals	☐ Vehicles	☐ Health
_____	☐ Friends	☐ Supernatural	☐ Hobbies
_____	☐ Relatives	☐ Technology	☐ Music
	☐ Traveling	☐ Nakedness	☐ Work

Date: _____ ☐   ☐   ☐   ☐   ☐   ☐   ☐
                         Sun   Mon   Tue   Wed   Thur   Fri   Sat

Feelings before sleep: _____

Quality of sleep: ☐ Good   ☐ Medium   ☐ Bad

Type of dream: ☐ Lucid   ☐ Nightmare
                     ☐ Positive   ☐ Other: _____

Have you had these dreams before?

               ☐ Yes   ☐ No
               ☐ Multiple   ☐ I don't know

Dream description: _____

_____

_____

_____

_____

_____

_____

Dream interpretation: _____

_____

_____

_____

_____

Time period of the dream:

☐ Past ☐ Present

☐ Future ☐ Unknown

Feelings present in the dream:

☐ Fear ☐ Anger ☐ Freedom ☐ Paralysis

☐ Happiness ☐ Sadness ☐ Panic ☐ Love

☐ Doubt ☐ Boredom ☐ Peace ☐ Vulnerability

☐ Luck ☐ Guilt ☐ Horror ☐ Disappointment

☐ Other: _____

The dream featured:

Symbols	Things	Colors	People	Places

Themes			
☐ Other:	☐ Home	☐ Weather	☐ Fire
_____	☐ Family	☐ Earth	☐ Water
_____	☐ Childhood	☐ Space	☐ Money
_____	☐ Animals	☐ Vehicles	☐ Health
_____	☐ Friends	☐ Supernatural	☐ Hobbies
	☐ Relatives	☐ Technology	☐ Music
	☐ Traveling	☐ Nakedness	☐ Work

···✿···

Date: _____ ☐   ☐   ☐   ☐   ☐   ☐   ☐
                         Sun   Mon   Tue   Wed   Thur   Fri   Sat

Feelings before sleep: _____

Quality of sleep: ☐ Good   ☐ Medium   ☐ Bad

Type of dream: ☐ Lucid   ☐ Nightmare
                    ☐ Positive   ☐ Other: _____

Have you had these dreams before?

                ☐ Yes   ☐ No
                ☐ Multiple ☐ I don't know

Dream description: _____

_____

_____

_____

_____

_____

_____

Dream interpretation:_____

_____

_____

_____

_____

···✿···

Time period of the dream: ☐ Past   ☐ Present

☐ Future   ☐ Unknown

Feelings present in the dream:

☐ Fear   ☐ Anger   ☐ Freedom   ☐ Paralysis

☐ Happiness   ☐ Sadness   ☐ Panic   ☐ Love

☐ Doubt   ☐ Boredom   ☐ Peace   ☐ Vulnerability

☐ Luck   ☐ Guilt   ☐ Horror   ☐ Disappointment

☐ Other: _____

The dream featured:

Symbols	Things	Colors	People	Places

Themes	☐ Home	☐ Weather	☐ Fire
☐ Other:	☐ Family	☐ Earth	☐ Water
_____	☐ Childhood	☐ Space	☐ Money
_____	☐ Animals	☐ Vehicles	☐ Health
_____	☐ Friends	☐ Supernatural	☐ Hobbies
_____	☐ Relatives	☐ Technology	☐ Music
	☐ Traveling	☐ Nakedness	☐ Work

···❁···

Date: _____ ☐   ☐   ☐   ☐   ☐   ☐   ☐
                       Sun   Mon   Tue   Wed   Thur   Fri   Sat

Feelings before sleep: _____

Quality of sleep: ☐ Good   ☐ Medium   ☐ Bad

Type of dream: ☐ Lucid   ☐ Nightmare
                       ☐ Positive   ☐ Other: _____

Have you had these dreams before?

               ☐ Yes   ☐ No
               ☐ Multiple   ☐ I don't know

Dream description: _____
_____
_____
_____
_____
_____
_____
_____

Dream interpretation: _____
_____
_____
_____
_____

···❁···

Time period of the dream: ☐ Past   ☐ Present

☐ Future   ☐ Unknown

Feelings present in the dream:

☐ Fear   ☐ Anger   ☐ Freedom   ☐ Paralysis

☐ Happiness   ☐ Sadness   ☐ Panic   ☐ Love

☐ Doubt   ☐ Boredom   ☐ Peace   ☐ Vulnerability

☐ Luck   ☐ Guilt   ☐ Horror   ☐ Disappointment

☐ Other: _____

The dream featured:

Symbols	Things	Colors	People	Places

Themes	☐ Home	☐ Weather	☐ Fire
☐ Other:	☐ Family	☐ Earth	☐ Water
_____	☐ Childhood	☐ Space	☐ Money
_____	☐ Animals	☐ Vehicles	☐ Health
_____	☐ Friends	☐ Supernatural	☐ Hobbies
_____	☐ Relatives	☐ Technology	☐ Music
_____	☐ Traveling	☐ Nakedness	☐ Work

Date: _____ ☐ ☐ ☐ ☐ ☐ ☐ ☐
　　　　　　　　　　　　Sun　Mon　Tue　Wed　Thur　Fri　Sat

Feelings before sleep: _____

Quality of sleep: ☐ Good ☐ Medium ☐ Bad

Type of dream: ☐ Lucid ☐ Nightmare
　　　　　　　　☐ Positive ☐ Other: _____

Have you had these dreams before?

☐ Yes ☐ No
☐ Multiple ☐ I don't know

Dream description: _____
_____
_____
_____
_____
_____
_____

Dream interpretation:_____
_____
_____
_____
_____

Time period of the dream: ☐ Past   ☐ Present

☐ Future   ☐ Unknown

Feelings present in the dream:

☐ Fear ☐ Anger ☐ Freedom ☐ Paralysis

☐ Happiness ☐ Sadness ☐ Panic ☐ Love

☐ Doubt ☐ Boredom ☐ Peace ☐ Vulnerability

☐ Luck ☐ Guilt ☐ Horror ☐ Disappointment

☐ Other: _____

The dream featured:

Symbols	Things	Colors	People	Places

Themes	☐ Home	☐ Weather	☐ Fire
☐ Other:	☐ Family	☐ Earth	☐ Water
_____	☐ Childhood	☐ Space	☐ Money
_____	☐ Animals	☐ Vehicles	☐ Health
_____	☐ Friends	☐ Supernatural	☐ Hobbies
_____	☐ Relatives	☐ Technology	☐ Music
	☐ Traveling	☐ Nakedness	☐ Work

····�֎····

Date: _____ ☐ ☐ ☐ ☐ ☐ ☐ ☐
                       Sun Mon Tue Wed Thur Fri Sat

Feelings before sleep: _____

Quality of sleep: ☐ Good   ☐ Medium   ☐ Bad

Type of dream: ☐ Lucid   ☐ Nightmare
                     ☐ Positive ☐ Other: _____

Have you had these dreams before?

                     ☐ Yes   ☐ No
                     ☐ Multiple ☐ I don't know

Dream description: _____
_____
_____
_____
_____
_____
_____
_____

Dream interpretation:_____
_____
_____
_____
_____

····✖····

Time period of the dream: ☐ Past   ☐ Present

☐ Future   ☐ Unknown

Feelings present in the dream:

☐ Fear   ☐ Anger   ☐ Freedom   ☐ Paralysis

☐ Happiness   ☐ Sadness   ☐ Panic   ☐ Love

☐ Doubt   ☐ Boredom   ☐ Peace   ☐ Vulnerability

☐ Luck   ☐ Guilt   ☐ Horror   ☐ Disappointment

☐ Other: _____

The dream featured:

Symbols	Things	Colors	People	Places

Themes	☐ Home	☐ Weather	☐ Fire
☐ Other:	☐ Family	☐ Earth	☐ Water
_____	☐ Childhood	☐ Space	☐ Money
_____	☐ Animals	☐ Vehicles	☐ Health
_____	☐ Friends	☐ Supernatural	☐ Hobbies
_____	☐ Relatives	☐ Technology	☐ Music
	☐ Traveling	☐ Nakedness	☐ Work

···❀···

Date: _____ ☐   ☐   ☐   ☐   ☐   ☐   ☐
                        Sun   Mon   Tue   Wed   Thur   Fri   Sat

Feelings before sleep: _____

Quality of sleep: ☐ Good   ☐ Medium   ☐ Bad

Type of dream: ☐ Lucid   ☐ Nightmare

                    ☐ Positive   ☐ Other: _____

Have you had these dreams before?

           ☐ Yes   ☐ No

           ☐ Multiple   ☐ I don't know

Dream description: _____

_____

_____

_____

_____

_____

_____

_____

Dream interpretation:_____

_____

_____

_____

_____

···❀···

Time period of the dream: ☐ Past ☐ Present

☐ Future ☐ Unknown

Feelings present in the dream:

☐ Fear   ☐ Anger   ☐ Freedom   ☐ Paralysis

☐ Happiness   ☐ Sadness   ☐ Panic   ☐ Love

☐ Doubt   ☐ Boredom   ☐ Peace   ☐ Vulnerability

☐ Luck   ☐ Guilt   ☐ Horror   ☐ Disappointment

☐ Other: _____

The dream featured:

Symbols	Things	Colors	People	Places

Themes	☐ Home	☐ Weather	☐ Fire
☐ Other:	☐ Family	☐ Earth	☐ Water
_____	☐ Childhood	☐ Space	☐ Money
_____	☐ Animals	☐ Vehicles	☐ Health
_____	☐ Friends	☐ Supernatural	☐ Hobbies
_____	☐ Relatives	☐ Technology	☐ Music
	☐ Traveling	☐ Nakedness	☐ Work

Date: _____ ☐   ☐   ☐   ☐   ☐   ☐   ☐
                   Sun   Mon   Tue   Wed   Thur   Fri   Sat

Feelings before sleep: _____

Quality of sleep: ☐ Good   ☐ Medium   ☐ Bad

Type of dream: ☐ Lucid   ☐ Nightmare
                 ☐ Positive   ☐ Other: _____

Have you had these dreams before?

                 ☐ Yes   ☐ No
                 ☐ Multiple   ☐ I don't know

Dream description: _____
_____
_____
_____
_____
_____
_____
_____

Dream interpretation:_____
_____
_____
_____
_____

Time period of the dream: ☐ Past ☐ Present

☐ Future ☐ Unknown

Feelings present in the dream:

☐ Fear ☐ Anger ☐ Freedom ☐ Paralysis

☐ Happiness ☐ Sadness ☐ Panic ☐ Love

☐ Doubt ☐ Boredom ☐ Peace ☐ Vulnerability

☐ Luck ☐ Guilt ☐ Horror ☐ Disappointment

☐ Other: _____

The dream featured:

Symbols	Things	Colors	People	Places

Themes			
☐ Other:	☐ Home	☐ Weather	☐ Fire
_____	☐ Family	☐ Earth	☐ Water
_____	☐ Childhood	☐ Space	☐ Money
_____	☐ Animals	☐ Vehicles	☐ Health
_____	☐ Friends	☐ Supernatural	☐ Hobbies
_____	☐ Relatives	☐ Technology	☐ Music
	☐ Traveling	☐ Nakedness	☐ Work

Date: _____ ☐ ☐ ☐ ☐ ☐ ☐ ☐
                              Sun Mon Tue Wed Thur Fri Sat

Feelings before sleep: _____

Quality of sleep: ☐ Good   ☐ Medium ☐ Bad

Type of dream: ☐ Lucid   ☐ Nightmare
                       ☐ Positive ☐ Other: _____

Have you had these dreams before?

        ☐ Yes   ☐ No
        ☐ Multiple ☐ I don't know

Dream description: _____

_____

_____

_____

_____

_____

_____

Dream interpretation: _____

_____

_____

_____

_____

Time period of the dream: ☐ Past   ☐ Present

                           ☐ Future   ☐ Unknown

Feelings present in the dream:

☐ Fear   ☐ Anger   ☐ Freedom   ☐ Paralysis

☐ Happiness   ☐ Sadness   ☐ Panic   ☐ Love

☐ Doubt   ☐ Boredom   ☐ Peace   ☐ Vulnerability

☐ Luck   ☐ Guilt   ☐ Horror   ☐ Disappointment

☐ Other: _____

The dream featured:

Symbols	Things	Colors	People	Places

Themes

☐ Other:

_____

_____

_____

_____

☐ Home   ☐ Weather   ☐ Fire

☐ Family   ☐ Earth   ☐ Water

☐ Childhood   ☐ Space   ☐ Money

☐ Animals   ☐ Vehicles   ☐ Health

☐ Friends   ☐ Supernatural   ☐ Hobbies

☐ Relatives   ☐ Technology   ☐ Music

☐ Traveling   ☐ Nakedness   ☐ Work

Date: _____ ☐   ☐   ☐   ☐   ☐   ☐   ☐
                        Sun   Mon   Tue   Wed   Thur   Fri   Sat

Feelings before sleep: _____

Quality of sleep: ☐ Good   ☐ Medium   ☐ Bad

Type of dream: ☐ Lucid   ☐ Nightmare

                     ☐ Positive   ☐ Other: _____

Have you had these dreams before?

         ☐ Yes   ☐ No

         ☐ Multiple   ☐ I don't know

Dream description: _____

_____

_____

_____

_____

_____

_____

_____

Dream interpretation:_____

_____

_____

_____

_____

_____

Time period of the dream: ☐ Past ☐ Present

☐ Future ☐ Unknown

Feelings present in the dream:

☐ Fear ☐ Anger ☐ Freedom ☐ Paralysis

☐ Happiness ☐ Sadness ☐ Panic ☐ Love

☐ Doubt ☐ Boredom ☐ Peace ☐ Vulnerability

☐ Luck ☐ Guilt ☐ Horror ☐ Disappointment

☐ Other: _____

The dream featured:

Symbols	Things	Colors	People	Places

Themes	☐ Home	☐ Weather	☐ Fire
☐ Other:	☐ Family	☐ Earth	☐ Water
_____	☐ Childhood	☐ Space	☐ Money
_____	☐ Animals	☐ Vehicles	☐ Health
_____	☐ Friends	☐ Supernatural	☐ Hobbies
_____	☐ Relatives	☐ Technology	☐ Music
	☐ Traveling	☐ Nakedness	☐ Work

Date: _____ ☐ ☐ ☐ ☐ ☐ ☐ ☐
                                   Sun Mon Tue Wed Thur Fri Sat

Feelings before sleep: _____

Quality of sleep: ☐ Good ☐ Medium ☐ Bad

Type of dream: ☐ Lucid ☐ Nightmare
                    ☐ Positive ☐ Other: _____

Have you had these dreams before?

                ☐ Yes ☐ No
                ☐ Multiple ☐ I don't know

Dream description: _____
_____
_____
_____
_____
_____
_____
_____

Dream interpretation:_____
_____
_____
_____
_____

Time period of the dream: ☐ Past ☐ Present

☐ Future ☐ Unknown

Feelings present in the dream:

☐ Fear ☐ Anger ☐ Freedom ☐ Paralysis

☐ Happiness ☐ Sadness ☐ Panic ☐ Love

☐ Doubt ☐ Boredom ☐ Peace ☐ Vulnerability

☐ Luck ☐ Guilt ☐ Horror ☐ Disappointment

☐ Other: _____

The dream featured:

Symbols	Things	Colors	People	Places

Themes	☐ Home	☐ Weather	☐ Fire
☐ Other:	☐ Family	☐ Earth	☐ Water
_____	☐ Childhood	☐ Space	☐ Money
_____	☐ Animals	☐ Vehicles	☐ Health
_____	☐ Friends	☐ Supernatural	☐ Hobbies
_____	☐ Relatives	☐ Technology	☐ Music
	☐ Traveling	☐ Nakedness	☐ Work

···❄···

Date: _____ ☐ ☐ ☐ ☐ ☐ ☐ ☐
　　　　　　　　　　　 Sun　Mon　Tue　Wed　Thur　Fri　Sat

Feelings before sleep: _____

Quality of sleep:　☐ Good　　☐ Medium　☐ Bad

Type of dream:　　☐ Lucid　　☐ Nightmare
　　　　　　　　　☐ Positive　☐ Other: _____

Have you had these dreams before?

　　　　　　　　☐ Yes　　☐ No
　　　　　　　　☐ Multiple　☐ I don't know

Dream description: _____
_____
_____
_____
_____
_____
_____
_____

Dream interpretation:_____
_____
_____
_____
_____

···❄···

Time period of the dream: ☐ Past ☐ Present

☐ Future ☐ Unknown

Feelings present in the dream:

☐ Fear ☐ Anger ☐ Freedom ☐ Paralysis

☐ Happiness ☐ Sadness ☐ Panic ☐ Love

☐ Doubt ☐ Boredom ☐ Peace ☐ Vulnerability

☐ Luck ☐ Guilt ☐ Horror ☐ Disappointment

☐ Other: _____

The dream featured:

Symbols	Things	Colors	People	Places

Themes	☐ Home	☐ Weather	☐ Fire
☐ Other:	☐ Family	☐ Earth	☐ Water
_____	☐ Childhood	☐ Space	☐ Money
_____	☐ Animals	☐ Vehicles	☐ Health
_____	☐ Friends	☐ Supernatural	☐ Hobbies
_____	☐ Relatives	☐ Technology	☐ Music
	☐ Traveling	☐ Nakedness	☐ Work

···�֎···

Date: _____ ☐ ☐ ☐ ☐ ☐ ☐ ☐
　　　　　　　　　　　Sun　Mon　Tue　Wed　Thur　Fri　Sat

Feelings before sleep: _____

Quality of sleep:　　☐ Good　　☐ Medium　☐ Bad

Type of dream:　　　☐ Lucid　　☐ Nightmare
　　　　　　　　　　☐ Positive　☐ Other: _____

Have you had these dreams before?

　　　　　　　　　☐ Yes　　☐ No
　　　　　　　　　☐ Multiple　☐ I don't know

Dream description: _____
_____
_____
_____
_____
_____
_____
_____

Dream interpretation:_____
_____
_____
_____
_____

···�֎···

Time period of the dream: ☐ Past ☐ Present

☐ Future ☐ Unknown

Feelings present in the dream:

☐ Fear ☐ Anger ☐ Freedom ☐ Paralysis

☐ Happiness ☐ Sadness ☐ Panic ☐ Love

☐ Doubt ☐ Boredom ☐ Peace ☐ Vulnerability

☐ Luck ☐ Guilt ☐ Horror ☐ Disappointment

☐ Other: _____

The dream featured:

Symbols	Things	Colors	People	Places

Themes	☐ Home	☐ Weather	☐ Fire
☐ Other:	☐ Family	☐ Earth	☐ Water
_____	☐ Childhood	☐ Space	☐ Money
_____	☐ Animals	☐ Vehicles	☐ Health
_____	☐ Friends	☐ Supernatural	☐ Hobbies
_____	☐ Relatives	☐ Technology	☐ Music
	☐ Traveling	☐ Nakedness	☐ Work

Date: _____ ☐ ☐ ☐ ☐ ☐ ☐ ☐
Sun Mon Tue Wed Thur Fri Sat

Feelings before sleep: _____

Quality of sleep: ☐ Good ☐ Medium ☐ Bad

Type of dream: ☐ Lucid ☐ Nightmare
☐ Positive ☐ Other: _____

Have you had these dreams before?

☐ Yes ☐ No
☐ Multiple ☐ I don't know

Dream description: _____
_____
_____
_____
_____
_____
_____
_____

Dream interpretation: _____
_____
_____
_____
_____

Time period of the dream: ☐ Past   ☐ Present

                           ☐ Future   ☐ Unknown

Feelings present in the dream:

☐ Fear   ☐ Anger   ☐ Freedom   ☐ Paralysis

☐ Happiness   ☐ Sadness   ☐ Panic   ☐ Love

☐ Doubt   ☐ Boredom   ☐ Peace   ☐ Vulnerability

☐ Luck   ☐ Guilt   ☐ Horror   ☐ Disappointment

☐ Other: _____

The dream featured:

Symbols	Things	Colors	People	Places

Themes	☐ Home	☐ Weather	☐ Fire
☐ Other:	☐ Family	☐ Earth	☐ Water
_____	☐ Childhood	☐ Space	☐ Money
_____	☐ Animals	☐ Vehicles	☐ Health
_____	☐ Friends	☐ Supernatural	☐ Hobbies
_____	☐ Relatives	☐ Technology	☐ Music
	☐ Traveling	☐ Nakedness	☐ Work

···❀···

Date: _____ ☐ ☐ ☐ ☐ ☐ ☐ ☐
Sun   Mon   Tue   Wed   Thur   Fri   Sat

Feelings before sleep: _____

Quality of sleep: ☐ Good   ☐ Medium   ☐ Bad

Type of dream: ☐ Lucid   ☐ Nightmare
                 ☐ Positive   ☐ Other: _____

Have you had these dreams before?

☐ Yes   ☐ No

☐ Multiple ☐ I don't know

Dream description: _____
_____
_____
_____
_____
_____
_____
_____

Dream interpretation: _____
_____
_____
_____
_____

···❀···

Time period of the dream: ☐ Past   ☐ Present

☐ Future   ☐ Unknown

Feelings present in the dream:

☐ Fear   ☐ Anger   ☐ Freedom   ☐ Paralysis

☐ Happiness   ☐ Sadness   ☐ Panic   ☐ Love

☐ Doubt   ☐ Boredom   ☐ Peace   ☐ Vulnerability

☐ Luck   ☐ Guilt   ☐ Horror   ☐ Disappointment

☐ Other: _____

The dream featured:

Symbols	Things	Colors	People	Places

Themes	☐ Home	☐ Weather	☐ Fire
☐ Other:	☐ Family	☐ Earth	☐ Water
_____	☐ Childhood	☐ Space	☐ Money
_____	☐ Animals	☐ Vehicles	☐ Health
_____	☐ Friends	☐ Supernatural	☐ Hobbies
_____	☐ Relatives	☐ Technology	☐ Music
	☐ Traveling	☐ Nakedness	☐ Work

Date: _____ ☐ ☐ ☐ ☐ ☐ ☐ ☐
 Sun Mon Tue Wed Thur Fri Sat

Feelings before sleep: _____

Quality of sleep: ☐ Good ☐ Medium ☐ Bad

Type of dream: ☐ Lucid ☐ Nightmare
 ☐ Positive ☐ Other: _____

Have you had these dreams before?

 ☐ Yes ☐ No
 ☐ Multiple ☐ I don't know

Dream description: _____
_____
_____
_____
_____
_____
_____
_____

Dream interpretation:_____
_____
_____
_____
_____

Time period of the dream: ☐ Past   ☐ Present

☐ Future   ☐ Unknown

Feelings present in the dream:

☐ Fear   ☐ Anger   ☐ Freedom   ☐ Paralysis

☐ Happiness   ☐ Sadness   ☐ Panic   ☐ Love

☐ Doubt   ☐ Boredom   ☐ Peace   ☐ Vulnerability

☐ Luck   ☐ Guilt   ☐ Horror   ☐ Disappointment

☐ Other: _____

The dream featured:

Symbols	Things	Colors	People	Places

Themes	☐ Home	☐ Weather	☐ Fire
☐ Other:	☐ Family	☐ Earth	☐ Water
_____	☐ Childhood	☐ Space	☐ Money
_____	☐ Animals	☐ Vehicles	☐ Health
_____	☐ Friends	☐ Supernatural	☐ Hobbies
_____	☐ Relatives	☐ Technology	☐ Music
	☐ Traveling	☐ Nakedness	☐ Work

Date: _____ ☐ ☐ ☐ ☐ ☐ ☐ ☐
                                     Sun Mon Tue Wed Thur Fri Sat

Feelings before sleep: _____

Quality of sleep: ☐ Good   ☐ Medium ☐ Bad

Type of dream: ☐ Lucid   ☐ Nightmare
                             ☐ Positive ☐ Other: _____

Have you had these dreams before?

                ☐ Yes   ☐ No
                ☐ Multiple ☐ I don't know

Dream description: _____

_____

_____

_____

_____

_____

_____

Dream interpretation:_____

_____

_____

_____

_____

Time period of the dream: ☐ Past   ☐ Present

☐ Future   ☐ Unknown

Feelings present in the dream:

☐ Fear   ☐ Anger   ☐ Freedom   ☐ Paralysis

☐ Happiness   ☐ Sadness   ☐ Panic   ☐ Love

☐ Doubt   ☐ Boredom   ☐ Peace   ☐ Vulnerability

☐ Luck   ☐ Guilt   ☐ Horror   ☐ Disappointment

☐ Other: _____

The dream featured:

Symbols	Things	Colors	People	Places

Themes			
☐ Other:	☐ Home	☐ Weather	☐ Fire
_____	☐ Family	☐ Earth	☐ Water
_____	☐ Childhood	☐ Space	☐ Money
_____	☐ Animals	☐ Vehicles	☐ Health
_____	☐ Friends	☐ Supernatural	☐ Hobbies
_____	☐ Relatives	☐ Technology	☐ Music
	☐ Traveling	☐ Nakedness	☐ Work

Date: _____ ☐ ☐ ☐ ☐ ☐ ☐ ☐
　　　　　　　　　　　Sun　Mon　Tue　Wed　Thur　Fri　Sat

Feelings before sleep: _____

Quality of sleep:　☐ Good　　☐ Medium　☐ Bad

Type of dream:　　☐ Lucid　　☐ Nightmare
　　　　　　　　　☐ Positive　☐ Other: _____

Have you had these dreams before?

　　　　　☐ Yes　　☐ No
　　　　　☐ Multiple　☐ I don't know

Dream description: _____
_____
_____
_____
_____
_____
_____
_____

Dream interpretation:_____
_____
_____
_____
_____

Time period of the dream: ☐ Past ☐ Present
                           ☐ Future ☐ Unknown

Feelings present in the dream:

☐ Fear   ☐ Anger   ☐ Freedom   ☐ Paralysis

☐ Happiness ☐ Sadness   ☐ Panic   ☐ Love

☐ Doubt   ☐ Boredom   ☐ Peace   ☐ Vulnerability

☐ Luck   ☐ Guilt   ☐ Horror   ☐ Disappointment

☐ Other: _____

The dream featured:

Symbols	Things	Colors	People	Places

Themes	☐ Home	☐ Weather	☐ Fire
☐ Other:	☐ Family	☐ Earth	☐ Water
_____	☐ Childhood	☐ Space	☐ Money
_____	☐ Animals	☐ Vehicles	☐ Health
_____	☐ Friends	☐ Supernatural	☐ Hobbies
_____	☐ Relatives	☐ Technology	☐ Music
	☐ Traveling	☐ Nakedness	☐ Work

❈

Date: _____ ☐ ☐ ☐ ☐ ☐ ☐ ☐
                                Sun Mon Tue Wed Thur Fri Sat

Feelings before sleep: _____

Quality of sleep: ☐ Good   ☐ Medium ☐ Bad

Type of dream: ☐ Lucid   ☐ Nightmare
                     ☐ Positive ☐ Other: _____

Have you had these dreams before?

              ☐ Yes   ☐ No
              ☐ Multiple ☐ I don't know

Dream description: _____
_____
_____
_____
_____
_____
_____
_____

Dream interpretation:_____
_____
_____
_____
_____

❈

Time period of the dream: ☐ Past   ☐ Present

                            ☐ Future ☐ Unknown

Feelings present in the dream:

☐ Fear   ☐ Anger   ☐ Freedom   ☐ Paralysis

☐ Happiness ☐ Sadness ☐ Panic   ☐ Love

☐ Doubt   ☐ Boredom ☐ Peace   ☐ Vulnerability

☐ Luck   ☐ Guilt   ☐ Horror   ☐ Disappointment

☐ Other: _____

The dream featured:

Symbols	Things	Colors	People	Places

Themes	☐ Home	☐ Weather	☐ Fire
☐ Other:	☐ Family	☐ Earth	☐ Water
_____	☐ Childhood	☐ Space	☐ Money
_____	☐ Animals	☐ Vehicles	☐ Health
_____	☐ Friends	☐ Supernatural	☐ Hobbies
_____	☐ Relatives	☐ Technology	☐ Music
	☐ Traveling	☐ Nakedness	☐ Work

···❁···

Date: _____ ☐ ☐ ☐ ☐ ☐ ☐ ☐
　　　　　　　　　　　 Sun　Mon　Tue　Wed　Thur　Fri　Sat

Feelings before sleep: _____

Quality of sleep: ☐ Good ☐ Medium ☐ Bad

Type of dream: ☐ Lucid ☐ Nightmare
　　　　　　　　 ☐ Positive ☐ Other: _____

Have you had these dreams before?

☐ Yes ☐ No
☐ Multiple ☐ I don't know

Dream description: _____
_____
_____
_____
_____
_____
_____
_____

Dream interpretation: _____
_____
_____
_____
_____

···❁···

Time period of the dream:
☐ Past ☐ Present
☐ Future ☐ Unknown

Feelings present in the dream:

☐ Fear ☐ Anger ☐ Freedom ☐ Paralysis

☐ Happiness ☐ Sadness ☐ Panic ☐ Love

☐ Doubt ☐ Boredom ☐ Peace ☐ Vulnerability

☐ Luck ☐ Guilt ☐ Horror ☐ Disappointment

☐ Other: _____

The dream featured:

Symbols	Things	Colors	People	Places

Themes	☐ Home	☐ Weather	☐ Fire
☐ Other:	☐ Family	☐ Earth	☐ Water
_____	☐ Childhood	☐ Space	☐ Money
_____	☐ Animals	☐ Vehicles	☐ Health
_____	☐ Friends	☐ Supernatural	☐ Hobbies
_____	☐ Relatives	☐ Technology	☐ Music
	☐ Traveling	☐ Nakedness	☐ Work

···❊···

Date: _____ ☐ ☐ ☐ ☐ ☐ ☐ ☐
Sun Mon Tue Wed Thur Fri Sat

Feelings before sleep: _____

Quality of sleep: ☐ Good ☐ Medium ☐ Bad

Type of dream: ☐ Lucid ☐ Nightmare
☐ Positive ☐ Other: _____

Have you had these dreams before?

☐ Yes ☐ No
☐ Multiple ☐ I don't know

Dream description: _____
_____
_____
_____
_____
_____
_____
_____

Dream interpretation: _____
_____
_____
_____
_____

···❊···

Time period of the dream: ☐ Past ☐ Present

☐ Future ☐ Unknown

Feelings present in the dream:

☐ Fear ☐ Anger ☐ Freedom ☐ Paralysis

☐ Happiness ☐ Sadness ☐ Panic ☐ Love

☐ Doubt ☐ Boredom ☐ Peace ☐ Vulnerability

☐ Luck ☐ Guilt ☐ Horror ☐ Disappointment

☐ Other: _____

The dream featured:

Symbols	Things	Colors	People	Places

Themes	☐ Home	☐ Weather	☐ Fire
☐ Other:	☐ Family	☐ Earth	☐ Water
_____	☐ Childhood	☐ Space	☐ Money
_____	☐ Animals	☐ Vehicles	☐ Health
_____	☐ Friends	☐ Supernatural	☐ Hobbies
_____	☐ Relatives	☐ Technology	☐ Music
	☐ Traveling	☐ Nakedness	☐ Work

Date: _____ ☐ ☐ ☐ ☐ ☐ ☐ ☐
　　　　　　　　　　　　Sun　Mon　Tue　Wed　Thur　Fri　Sat

Feelings before sleep: _____

Quality of sleep:　　☐ Good　　　☐ Medium　☐ Bad

Type of dream:　　　☐ Lucid　　　☐ Nightmare
　　　　　　　　　　☐ Positive　　☐ Other: _____

Have you had these dreams before?

　　　　　　　　　　☐ Yes　　　☐ No
　　　　　　　　　　☐ Multiple　☐ I don't know

Dream description: _____
_____
_____
_____
_____
_____
_____
_____

Dream interpretation:_____
_____
_____
_____
_____

Time period of the dream: ☐ Past   ☐ Present

☐ Future   ☐ Unknown

Feelings present in the dream:

☐ Fear   ☐ Anger   ☐ Freedom   ☐ Paralysis

☐ Happiness   ☐ Sadness   ☐ Panic   ☐ Love

☐ Doubt   ☐ Boredom   ☐ Peace   ☐ Vulnerability

☐ Luck   ☐ Guilt   ☐ Horror   ☐ Disappointment

☐ Other: _____

The dream featured:

Symbols	Things	Colors	People	Places

Themes	☐ Home	☐ Weather	☐ Fire
☐ Other:	☐ Family	☐ Earth	☐ Water
_____	☐ Childhood	☐ Space	☐ Money
_____	☐ Animals	☐ Vehicles	☐ Health
_____	☐ Friends	☐ Supernatural	☐ Hobbies
_____	☐ Relatives	☐ Technology	☐ Music
	☐ Traveling	☐ Nakedness	☐ Work

Date: _____ ☐ ☐ ☐ ☐ ☐ ☐ ☐
                      Sun Mon Tue Wed Thur Fri Sat

Feelings before sleep: _____

Quality of sleep: ☐ Good   ☐ Medium   ☐ Bad

Type of dream: ☐ Lucid   ☐ Nightmare
                      ☐ Positive ☐ Other: _____

Have you had these dreams before?

                      ☐ Yes   ☐ No
                      ☐ Multiple ☐ I don't know

Dream description: _____
_____
_____
_____
_____
_____
_____
_____

Dream interpretation: _____
_____
_____
_____
_____

Time period of the dream:　　　　□ Past　　　□ Present

□ Future　　□ Unknown

Feelings present in the dream:

□ Fear　　　　□ Anger　　　□ Freedom　　□ Paralysis

□ Happiness　□ Sadness　　□ Panic　　　□ Love

□ Doubt　　　□ Boredom　　□ Peace　　　□ Vulnerability

□ Luck　　　　□ Guilt　　　□ Horror　　　□ Disappointment

□ Other: _____

The dream featured:

Symbols	Things	Colors	People	Places

Themes	□ Home	□ Weather	□ Fire
□ Other:	□ Family	□ Earth	□ Water
_____	□ Childhood	□ Space	□ Money
_____	□ Animals	□ Vehicles	□ Health
_____	□ Friends	□ Supernatural	□ Hobbies
_____	□ Relatives	□ Technology	□ Music
	□ Traveling	□ Nakedness	□ Work

Date: _____ ☐ ☐ ☐ ☐ ☐ ☐ ☐
                            Sun Mon Tue Wed Thur Fri Sat

Feelings before sleep: _____

Quality of sleep: ☐ Good   ☐ Medium ☐ Bad

Type of dream: ☐ Lucid   ☐ Nightmare
                       ☐ Positive ☐ Other: _____

Have you had these dreams before?

          ☐ Yes   ☐ No
          ☐ Multiple ☐ I don't know

Dream description: _____
_____
_____
_____
_____
_____
_____

Dream interpretation: _____
_____
_____
_____
_____

Time period of the dream: ☐ Past ☐ Present

☐ Future ☐ Unknown

Feelings present in the dream:

☐ Fear ☐ Anger ☐ Freedom ☐ Paralysis

☐ Happiness ☐ Sadness ☐ Panic ☐ Love

☐ Doubt ☐ Boredom ☐ Peace ☐ Vulnerability

☐ Luck ☐ Guilt ☐ Horror ☐ Disappointment

☐ Other: _____

The dream featured:

Symbols	Things	Colors	People	Places

Themes	☐ Home	☐ Weather	☐ Fire
☐ Other:	☐ Family	☐ Earth	☐ Water
_____	☐ Childhood	☐ Space	☐ Money
_____	☐ Animals	☐ Vehicles	☐ Health
_____	☐ Friends	☐ Supernatural	☐ Hobbies
_____	☐ Relatives	☐ Technology	☐ Music
	☐ Traveling	☐ Nakedness	☐ Work

Date: _____ ☐ ☐ ☐ ☐ ☐ ☐ ☐
　　　　　　　　　　　Sun　Mon　Tue　Wed　Thur　Fri　Sat

Feelings before sleep: _____

Quality of sleep:　☐ Good　　☐ Medium　☐ Bad

Type of dream:　☐ Lucid　　☐ Nightmare
　　　　　　　　☐ Positive　☐ Other: _____

Have you had these dreams before?

　　　　　　☐ Yes　　☐ No
　　　　　　☐ Multiple　☐ I don't know

Dream description: _____
_____
_____
_____
_____
_____
_____
_____

Dream interpretation:_____
_____
_____
_____
_____

Time period of the dream: ☐ Past   ☐ Present

☐ Future   ☐ Unknown

Feelings present in the dream:

☐ Fear   ☐ Anger   ☐ Freedom   ☐ Paralysis

☐ Happiness   ☐ Sadness   ☐ Panic   ☐ Love

☐ Doubt   ☐ Boredom   ☐ Peace   ☐ Vulnerability

☐ Luck   ☐ Guilt   ☐ Horror   ☐ Disappointment

☐ Other: _____

The dream featured:

Symbols	Things	Colors	People	Places

Themes	☐ Home	☐ Weather	☐ Fire
☐ Other:	☐ Family	☐ Earth	☐ Water
_____	☐ Childhood	☐ Space	☐ Money
_____	☐ Animals	☐ Vehicles	☐ Health
_____	☐ Friends	☐ Supernatural	☐ Hobbies
_____	☐ Relatives	☐ Technology	☐ Music
	☐ Traveling	☐ Nakedness	☐ Work

Date: _____ ☐ ☐ ☐ ☐ ☐ ☐ ☐
　　　　　　　　　　　 Sun　Mon　Tue　Wed　Thur　Fri　Sat

Feelings before sleep: _____

Quality of sleep: 　☐ Good 　　☐ Medium 　☐ Bad

Type of dream: 　　☐ Lucid 　　☐ Nightmare
　　　　　　　　　☐ Positive 　☐ Other: _____

Have you had these dreams before?

　　　　　　　　☐ Yes 　　☐ No
　　　　　　　　☐ Multiple 　☐ I don't know

Dream description: _____
_____
_____
_____
_____
_____
_____
_____

Dream interpretation: _____
_____
_____
_____
_____

Time period of the dream: ☐ Past ☐ Present
                           ☐ Future ☐ Unknown

Feelings present in the dream:

☐ Fear   ☐ Anger   ☐ Freedom   ☐ Paralysis

☐ Happiness ☐ Sadness   ☐ Panic   ☐ Love

☐ Doubt   ☐ Boredom   ☐ Peace   ☐ Vulnerability

☐ Luck   ☐ Guilt   ☐ Horror   ☐ Disappointment

☐ Other: _____

The dream featured:

Symbols	Things	Colors	People	Places

Themes			
☐ Other:	☐ Home	☐ Weather	☐ Fire
_____	☐ Family	☐ Earth	☐ Water
_____	☐ Childhood	☐ Space	☐ Money
_____	☐ Animals	☐ Vehicles	☐ Health
_____	☐ Friends	☐ Supernatural	☐ Hobbies
_____	☐ Relatives	☐ Technology	☐ Music
	☐ Traveling	☐ Nakedness	☐ Work

Date: ______________ ☐ Sun ☐ Mon ☐ Tue ☐ Wed ☐ Thur ☐ Fri ☐ Sat

Feelings before sleep: ______________________________

Quality of sleep: ☐ Good ☐ Medium ☐ Bad

Type of dream: ☐ Lucid ☐ Nightmare

☐ Positive ☐ Other: ______________

Have you had these dreams before?

☐ Yes ☐ No

☐ Multiple ☐ I don't know

Dream description: ______________________________

Dream interpretation: ______________________________

Time period of the dream: ☐ Past   ☐ Present

☐ Future   ☐ Unknown

Feelings present in the dream:

☐ Fear   ☐ Anger   ☐ Freedom   ☐ Paralysis

☐ Happiness   ☐ Sadness   ☐ Panic   ☐ Love

☐ Doubt   ☐ Boredom   ☐ Peace   ☐ Vulnerability

☐ Luck   ☐ Guilt   ☐ Horror   ☐ Disappointment

☐ Other: _____

The dream featured:

Symbols	Things	Colors	People	Places

Themes	☐ Home	☐ Weather	☐ Fire
☐ Other:	☐ Family	☐ Earth	☐ Water
_____	☐ Childhood	☐ Space	☐ Money
_____	☐ Animals	☐ Vehicles	☐ Health
_____	☐ Friends	☐ Supernatural	☐ Hobbies
_____	☐ Relatives	☐ Technology	☐ Music
	☐ Traveling	☐ Nakedness	☐ Work

Date: _____ ☐ ☐ ☐ ☐ ☐ ☐ ☐
                               Sun   Mon   Tue   Wed   Thur   Fri   Sat

Feelings before sleep: _____

Quality of sleep: ☐ Good   ☐ Medium   ☐ Bad

Type of dream: ☐ Lucid   ☐ Nightmare
                          ☐ Positive   ☐ Other: _____

Have you had these dreams before?

             ☐ Yes   ☐ No
             ☐ Multiple ☐ I don't know

Dream description: _____
_____
_____
_____
_____
_____
_____
_____

Dream interpretation:_____
_____
_____
_____
_____

Time period of the dream: ☐ Past   ☐ Present

                             ☐ Future   ☐ Unknown

Feelings present in the dream:

☐ Fear   ☐ Anger   ☐ Freedom   ☐ Paralysis

☐ Happiness   ☐ Sadness   ☐ Panic   ☐ Love

☐ Doubt   ☐ Boredom   ☐ Peace   ☐ Vulnerability

☐ Luck   ☐ Guilt   ☐ Horror   ☐ Disappointment

☐ Other: _____

The dream featured:

Symbols	Things	Colors	People	Places

Themes	☐ Home	☐ Weather	☐ Fire
☐ Other:	☐ Family	☐ Earth	☐ Water
_____	☐ Childhood	☐ Space	☐ Money
_____	☐ Animals	☐ Vehicles	☐ Health
_____	☐ Friends	☐ Supernatural	☐ Hobbies
_____	☐ Relatives	☐ Technology	☐ Music
	☐ Traveling	☐ Nakedness	☐ Work

···�֎···

Date: _____ ☐ ☐ ☐ ☐ ☐ ☐ ☐
                               Sun   Mon   Tue   Wed Thur Fri   Sat

Feelings before sleep: _____

Quality of sleep: ☐ Good   ☐ Medium ☐ Bad

Type of dream: ☐ Lucid   ☐ Nightmare
                          ☐ Positive ☐ Other: _____

Have you had these dreams before?

               ☐ Yes   ☐ No
               ☐ Multiple ☐ I don't know

Dream description: _____
_____
_____
_____
_____
_____
_____
_____

Dream interpretation: _____
_____
_____
_____
_____

···�֎···

Time period of the dream: ☐ Past   ☐ Present

☐ Future   ☐ Unknown

Feelings present in the dream:

☐ Fear   ☐ Anger   ☐ Freedom   ☐ Paralysis

☐ Happiness   ☐ Sadness   ☐ Panic   ☐ Love

☐ Doubt   ☐ Boredom   ☐ Peace   ☐ Vulnerability

☐ Luck   ☐ Guilt   ☐ Horror   ☐ Disappointment

☐ Other: _____

The dream featured:

Symbols	Things	Colors	People	Places

Themes	☐ Home	☐ Weather	☐ Fire
☐ Other:	☐ Family	☐ Earth	☐ Water
_____	☐ Childhood	☐ Space	☐ Money
_____	☐ Animals	☐ Vehicles	☐ Health
_____	☐ Friends	☐ Supernatural	☐ Hobbies
_____	☐ Relatives	☐ Technology	☐ Music
	☐ Traveling	☐ Nakedness	☐ Work

Date: _____ ☐   ☐   ☐   ☐   ☐   ☐   ☐
                       Sun   Mon   Tue   Wed   Thur   Fri   Sat

Feelings before sleep: _____

Quality of sleep: ☐ Good   ☐ Medium   ☐ Bad

Type of dream: ☐ Lucid   ☐ Nightmare

                    ☐ Positive   ☐ Other: _____

Have you had these dreams before?

                  ☐ Yes   ☐ No

                  ☐ Multiple   ☐ I don't know

Dream description: _____

_____

_____

_____

_____

_____

_____

_____

Dream interpretation: _____

_____

_____

_____

_____

Time period of the dream: □ Past   □ Present

                          □ Future   □ Unknown

Feelings present in the dream:

□ Fear   □ Anger   □ Freedom   □ Paralysis

□ Happiness   □ Sadness   □ Panic   □ Love

□ Doubt   □ Boredom   □ Peace   □ Vulnerability

□ Luck   □ Guilt   □ Horror   □ Disappointment

□ Other: _____

The dream featured:

Symbols	Things	Colors	People	Places

Themes	□ Home	□ Weather	□ Fire
□ Other:	□ Family	□ Earth	□ Water
_____	□ Childhood	□ Space	□ Money
_____	□ Animals	□ Vehicles	□ Health
_____	□ Friends	□ Supernatural	□ Hobbies
_____	□ Relatives	□ Technology	□ Music
	□ Traveling	□ Nakedness	□ Work

Date: _____ ☐   ☐   ☐   ☐   ☐   ☐   ☐
                    Sun   Mon   Tue   Wed   Thur   Fri   Sat

Feelings before sleep: _____

Quality of sleep: ☐ Good   ☐ Medium   ☐ Bad

Type of dream: ☐ Lucid   ☐ Nightmare
                      ☐ Positive   ☐ Other: _____

Have you had these dreams before?

                 ☐ Yes   ☐ No
                 ☐ Multiple   ☐ I don't know

Dream description: _____

_____

_____

_____

_____

_____

_____

_____

Dream interpretation:_____

_____

_____

_____

_____

Time period of the dream: ☐ Past   ☐ Present

                            ☐ Future   ☐ Unknown

Feelings present in the dream:

☐ Fear   ☐ Anger   ☐ Freedom   ☐ Paralysis

☐ Happiness   ☐ Sadness   ☐ Panic   ☐ Love

☐ Doubt   ☐ Boredom   ☐ Peace   ☐ Vulnerability

☐ Luck   ☐ Guilt   ☐ Horror   ☐ Disappointment

☐ Other: _____

The dream featured:

Symbols	Things	Colors	People	Places

Themes	☐ Home	☐ Weather	☐ Fire
☐ Other:	☐ Family	☐ Earth	☐ Water
_____	☐ Childhood	☐ Space	☐ Money
_____	☐ Animals	☐ Vehicles	☐ Health
_____	☐ Friends	☐ Supernatural	☐ Hobbies
_____	☐ Relatives	☐ Technology	☐ Music
	☐ Traveling	☐ Nakedness	☐ Work

Date: _____ ☐   ☐   ☐   ☐   ☐   ☐   ☐
                             Sun   Mon   Tue   Wed   Thur   Fri   Sat

Feelings before sleep: _____

Quality of sleep: ☐ Good   ☐ Medium   ☐ Bad

Type of dream: ☐ Lucid   ☐ Nightmare
                        ☐ Positive   ☐ Other: _____

Have you had these dreams before?

               ☐ Yes   ☐ No
               ☐ Multiple   ☐ I don't know

Dream description: _____
_____
_____
_____
_____
_____
_____
_____

Dream interpretation:_____
_____
_____
_____
_____

Time period of the dream: ☐ Past ☐ Present

☐ Future ☐ Unknown

Feelings present in the dream:

☐ Fear ☐ Anger ☐ Freedom ☐ Paralysis

☐ Happiness ☐ Sadness ☐ Panic ☐ Love

☐ Doubt ☐ Boredom ☐ Peace ☐ Vulnerability

☐ Luck ☐ Guilt ☐ Horror ☐ Disappointment

☐ Other: _____

The dream featured:

Symbols	Things	Colors	People	Places

Themes	☐ Home	☐ Weather	☐ Fire
☐ Other:	☐ Family	☐ Earth	☐ Water
_____	☐ Childhood	☐ Space	☐ Money
_____	☐ Animals	☐ Vehicles	☐ Health
_____	☐ Friends	☐ Supernatural	☐ Hobbies
_____	☐ Relatives	☐ Technology	☐ Music
	☐ Traveling	☐ Nakedness	☐ Work

Date: _____ ☐ ☐ ☐ ☐ ☐ ☐ ☐
                     Sun Mon Tue Wed Thur Fri Sat

Feelings before sleep: _____

Quality of sleep: ☐ Good   ☐ Medium   ☐ Bad

Type of dream: ☐ Lucid   ☐ Nightmare
                     ☐ Positive ☐ Other: _____

Have you had these dreams before?

        ☐ Yes   ☐ No
        ☐ Multiple ☐ I don't know

Dream description: _____
_____
_____
_____
_____
_____
_____
_____

Dream interpretation:_____
_____
_____
_____
_____

Time period of the dream: ☐ Past ☐ Present

☐ Future ☐ Unknown

Feelings present in the dream:

☐ Fear ☐ Anger ☐ Freedom ☐ Paralysis

☐ Happiness ☐ Sadness ☐ Panic ☐ Love

☐ Doubt ☐ Boredom ☐ Peace ☐ Vulnerability

☐ Luck ☐ Guilt ☐ Horror ☐ Disappointment

☐ Other: _____

The dream featured:

Symbols	Things	Colors	People	Places

Themes	☐ Home	☐ Weather	☐ Fire
☐ Other:	☐ Family	☐ Earth	☐ Water
_____	☐ Childhood	☐ Space	☐ Money
_____	☐ Animals	☐ Vehicles	☐ Health
_____	☐ Friends	☐ Supernatural	☐ Hobbies
_____	☐ Relatives	☐ Technology	☐ Music
	☐ Traveling	☐ Nakedness	☐ Work

Date: _____ ☐ ☐ ☐ ☐ ☐ ☐ ☐
Sun Mon Tue Wed Thur Fri Sat

Feelings before sleep: _____

Quality of sleep: ☐ Good   ☐ Medium   ☐ Bad

Type of dream: ☐ Lucid   ☐ Nightmare
                    ☐ Positive   ☐ Other: _____

Have you had these dreams before?

          ☐ Yes   ☐ No
          ☐ Multiple   ☐ I don't know

Dream description: _____
_____
_____
_____
_____
_____
_____
_____

Dream interpretation:_____
_____
_____
_____
_____

Time period of the dream: ☐ Past   ☐ Present

☐ Future   ☐ Unknown

Feelings present in the dream:

☐ Fear   ☐ Anger   ☐ Freedom   ☐ Paralysis

☐ Happiness   ☐ Sadness   ☐ Panic   ☐ Love

☐ Doubt   ☐ Boredom   ☐ Peace   ☐ Vulnerability

☐ Luck   ☐ Guilt   ☐ Horror   ☐ Disappointment

☐ Other: _____

The dream featured:

Symbols	Things	Colors	People	Places

Themes	☐ Home	☐ Weather	☐ Fire
☐ Other:	☐ Family	☐ Earth	☐ Water
_____	☐ Childhood	☐ Space	☐ Money
_____	☐ Animals	☐ Vehicles	☐ Health
_____	☐ Friends	☐ Supernatural	☐ Hobbies
_____	☐ Relatives	☐ Technology	☐ Music
	☐ Traveling	☐ Nakedness	☐ Work

Date: _____ ☐ ☐ ☐ ☐ ☐ ☐ ☐
                        Sun   Mon   Tue   Wed   Thur   Fri   Sat

Feelings before sleep: _____

Quality of sleep: ☐ Good   ☐ Medium   ☐ Bad

Type of dream: ☐ Lucid   ☐ Nightmare
                      ☐ Positive ☐ Other: _____

Have you had these dreams before?

                      ☐ Yes   ☐ No
                      ☐ Multiple ☐ I don't know

Dream description: _____
_____
_____
_____
_____
_____
_____
_____

Dream interpretation: _____
_____
_____
_____
_____

Time period of the dream: ☐ Past   ☐ Present

                          ☐ Future   ☐ Unknown

Feelings present in the dream:

☐ Fear   ☐ Anger   ☐ Freedom   ☐ Paralysis

☐ Happiness   ☐ Sadness   ☐ Panic   ☐ Love

☐ Doubt   ☐ Boredom   ☐ Peace   ☐ Vulnerability

☐ Luck   ☐ Guilt   ☐ Horror   ☐ Disappointment

☐ Other: _____

The dream featured:

Symbols	Things	Colors	People	Places

Themes	☐ Home	☐ Weather	☐ Fire
☐ Other:	☐ Family	☐ Earth	☐ Water
_____	☐ Childhood	☐ Space	☐ Money
_____	☐ Animals	☐ Vehicles	☐ Health
_____	☐ Friends	☐ Supernatural	☐ Hobbies
_____	☐ Relatives	☐ Technology	☐ Music
	☐ Traveling	☐ Nakedness	☐ Work

Date: _____ ☐ ☐ ☐ ☐ ☐ ☐ ☐
　　　　　　　　　　Sun　Mon　Tue　Wed　Thur　Fri　Sat

Feelings before sleep: _____

Quality of sleep: ☐ Good ☐ Medium ☐ Bad

Type of dream: ☐ Lucid ☐ Nightmare
　　　　　　　 ☐ Positive ☐ Other: _____

Have you had these dreams before?

☐ Yes ☐ No
☐ Multiple ☐ I don't know

Dream description: _____
_____
_____
_____
_____
_____
_____

Dream interpretation: _____
_____
_____
_____
_____

Time period of the dream: ☐ Past   ☐ Present

☐ Future   ☐ Unknown

Feelings present in the dream:

☐ Fear   ☐ Anger   ☐ Freedom   ☐ Paralysis

☐ Happiness   ☐ Sadness   ☐ Panic   ☐ Love

☐ Doubt   ☐ Boredom   ☐ Peace   ☐ Vulnerability

☐ Luck   ☐ Guilt   ☐ Horror   ☐ Disappointment

☐ Other: _____

The dream featured:

Symbols	Things	Colors	People	Places

Themes	☐ Home	☐ Weather	☐ Fire
☐ Other:	☐ Family	☐ Earth	☐ Water
_____	☐ Childhood	☐ Space	☐ Money
_____	☐ Animals	☐ Vehicles	☐ Health
_____	☐ Friends	☐ Supernatural	☐ Hobbies
_____	☐ Relatives	☐ Technology	☐ Music
	☐ Traveling	☐ Nakedness	☐ Work

···❈···

Date: _____ ☐ ☐ ☐ ☐ ☐ ☐ ☐
Sun Mon Tue Wed Thur Fri Sat

Feelings before sleep: _____

Quality of sleep: ☐ Good ☐ Medium ☐ Bad

Type of dream: ☐ Lucid ☐ Nightmare
☐ Positive ☐ Other: _____

Have you had these dreams before?

☐ Yes ☐ No
☐ Multiple ☐ I don't know

Dream description: _____
_____
_____
_____
_____
_____
_____
_____

Dream interpretation: _____
_____
_____
_____
_____

···❈···

Time period of the dream: ☐ Past ☐ Present

☐ Future ☐ Unknown

Feelings present in the dream:

☐ Fear ☐ Anger ☐ Freedom ☐ Paralysis

☐ Happiness ☐ Sadness ☐ Panic ☐ Love

☐ Doubt ☐ Boredom ☐ Peace ☐ Vulnerability

☐ Luck ☐ Guilt ☐ Horror ☐ Disappointment

☐ Other: _____

The dream featured:

Symbols	Things	Colors	People	Places

Themes	☐ Home	☐ Weather	☐ Fire
☐ Other:	☐ Family	☐ Earth	☐ Water
_____	☐ Childhood	☐ Space	☐ Money
_____	☐ Animals	☐ Vehicles	☐ Health
_____	☐ Friends	☐ Supernatural	☐ Hobbies
_____	☐ Relatives	☐ Technology	☐ Music
	☐ Traveling	☐ Nakedness	☐ Work

Date: _____ ☐ ☐ ☐ ☐ ☐ ☐ ☐
                     Sun Mon Tue Wed Thur Fri Sat

Feelings before sleep: _____

Quality of sleep: ☐ Good   ☐ Medium   ☐ Bad

Type of dream: ☐ Lucid   ☐ Nightmare
                   ☐ Positive   ☐ Other: _____

Have you had these dreams before?

                   ☐ Yes   ☐ No
                   ☐ Multiple ☐ I don't know

Dream description: _____
_____
_____
_____
_____
_____
_____
_____

Dream interpretation:_____
_____
_____
_____
_____

Time period of the dream: ☐ Past ☐ Present ☐ Future ☐ Unknown

Feelings present in the dream:

☐ Fear ☐ Anger ☐ Freedom ☐ Paralysis

☐ Happiness ☐ Sadness ☐ Panic ☐ Love

☐ Doubt ☐ Boredom ☐ Peace ☐ Vulnerability

☐ Luck ☐ Guilt ☐ Horror ☐ Disappointment

☐ Other: _____

The dream featured:

Symbols	Things	Colors	People	Places

Themes	☐ Home	☐ Weather	☐ Fire
☐ Other:	☐ Family	☐ Earth	☐ Water
_____	☐ Childhood	☐ Space	☐ Money
_____	☐ Animals	☐ Vehicles	☐ Health
_____	☐ Friends	☐ Supernatural	☐ Hobbies
_____	☐ Relatives	☐ Technology	☐ Music
	☐ Traveling	☐ Nakedness	☐ Work

···✤···

Date: _____ ☐ ☐ ☐ ☐ ☐ ☐ ☐
　　　　　　　　　　　Sun　Mon　Tue　Wed　Thur　Fri　Sat

Feelings before sleep: _____

Quality of sleep:　☐ Good　　☐ Medium　☐ Bad

Type of dream:　☐ Lucid　　☐ Nightmare
　　　　　　　　☐ Positive　☐ Other: _____

Have you had these dreams before?

　　　　　　☐ Yes　　☐ No
　　　　　　☐ Multiple　☐ I don't know

Dream description: _____

_____
_____
_____
_____
_____
_____
_____

Dream interpretation:_____

_____
_____
_____
_____

···✤···

Time period of the dream: □ Past □ Present

□ Future □ Unknown

Feelings present in the dream:

□ Fear □ Anger □ Freedom □ Paralysis

□ Happiness □ Sadness □ Panic □ Love

□ Doubt □ Boredom □ Peace □ Vulnerability

□ Luck □ Guilt □ Horror □ Disappointment

□ Other: _____

The dream featured:

Symbols	Things	Colors	People	Places

Themes	□ Home	□ Weather	□ Fire
□ Other:	□ Family	□ Earth	□ Water
_____	□ Childhood	□ Space	□ Money
_____	□ Animals	□ Vehicles	□ Health
_____	□ Friends	□ Supernatural	□ Hobbies
_____	□ Relatives	□ Technology	□ Music
	□ Traveling	□ Nakedness	□ Work

Date: _____ ☐ ☐ ☐ ☐ ☐ ☐ ☐
　　　　　　　　　　　 Sun　Mon　Tue　Wed　Thur　Fri　Sat

Feelings before sleep: _____

Quality of sleep:　　☐ Good　　☐ Medium　☐ Bad

Type of dream:　　　☐ Lucid　　☐ Nightmare
　　　　　　　　　　☐ Positive　☐ Other: _____

Have you had these dreams before?

　　　　　　　　　☐ Yes　　　☐ No
　　　　　　　　　☐ Multiple　☐ I don't know

Dream description: _____
_____
_____
_____
_____
_____
_____
_____

Dream interpretation:_____
_____
_____
_____
_____

Time period of the dream: ☐ Past ☐ Present

☐ Future ☐ Unknown

Feelings present in the dream:

☐ Fear ☐ Anger ☐ Freedom ☐ Paralysis

☐ Happiness ☐ Sadness ☐ Panic ☐ Love

☐ Doubt ☐ Boredom ☐ Peace ☐ Vulnerability

☐ Luck ☐ Guilt ☐ Horror ☐ Disappointment

☐ Other: _____

The dream featured:

Symbols	Things	Colors	People	Places

Themes	☐ Home	☐ Weather	☐ Fire
☐ Other:	☐ Family	☐ Earth	☐ Water
_____	☐ Childhood	☐ Space	☐ Money
_____	☐ Animals	☐ Vehicles	☐ Health
_____	☐ Friends	☐ Supernatural	☐ Hobbies
_____	☐ Relatives	☐ Technology	☐ Music
	☐ Traveling	☐ Nakedness	☐ Work

Date: _____ ☐ ☐ ☐ ☐ ☐ ☐ ☐
                    Sun Mon Tue Wed Thur Fri Sat

Feelings before sleep: _____

Quality of sleep: ☐ Good   ☐ Medium   ☐ Bad

Type of dream: ☐ Lucid   ☐ Nightmare
                      ☐ Positive ☐ Other: _____

Have you had these dreams before?

              ☐ Yes   ☐ No
              ☐ Multiple   ☐ I don't know

Dream description: _____
_____
_____
_____
_____
_____
_____
_____

Dream interpretation: _____
_____
_____
_____
_____

Time period of the dream: ☐ Past   ☐ Present

                            ☐ Future   ☐ Unknown

Feelings present in the dream:

☐ Fear   ☐ Anger   ☐ Freedom   ☐ Paralysis

☐ Happiness ☐ Sadness ☐ Panic   ☐ Love

☐ Doubt   ☐ Boredom ☐ Peace   ☐ Vulnerability

☐ Luck   ☐ Guilt   ☐ Horror   ☐ Disappointment

☐ Other: _____

The dream featured:

Symbols	Things	Colors	People	Places

Themes	☐ Home	☐ Weather	☐ Fire
☐ Other:	☐ Family	☐ Earth	☐ Water
_____	☐ Childhood	☐ Space	☐ Money
_____	☐ Animals	☐ Vehicles	☐ Health
_____	☐ Friends	☐ Supernatural	☐ Hobbies
_____	☐ Relatives	☐ Technology	☐ Music
	☐ Traveling	☐ Nakedness	☐ Work

···❂···

Date: _____ ☐   ☐   ☐   ☐   ☐   ☐   ☐
                           Sun   Mon   Tue   Wed   Thur   Fri   Sat

Feelings before sleep: _____

Quality of sleep: ☐ Good   ☐ Medium   ☐ Bad

Type of dream: ☐ Lucid   ☐ Nightmare
                     ☐ Positive   ☐ Other: _____

Have you had these dreams before?

                 ☐ Yes   ☐ No
                 ☐ Multiple   ☐ I don't know

Dream description: _____

_____

_____

_____

_____

_____

_____

_____

Dream interpretation:_____

_____

_____

_____

_____

···❂···

Time period of the dream: ☐ Past ☐ Present
☐ Future ☐ Unknown

Feelings present in the dream:

☐ Fear ☐ Anger ☐ Freedom ☐ Paralysis

☐ Happiness ☐ Sadness ☐ Panic ☐ Love

☐ Doubt ☐ Boredom ☐ Peace ☐ Vulnerability

☐ Luck ☐ Guilt ☐ Horror ☐ Disappointment

☐ Other: _____

The dream featured:

Symbols	Things	Colors	People	Places

Themes	☐ Home	☐ Weather	☐ Fire
☐ Other:	☐ Family	☐ Earth	☐ Water
_____	☐ Childhood	☐ Space	☐ Money
_____	☐ Animals	☐ Vehicles	☐ Health
_____	☐ Friends	☐ Supernatural	☐ Hobbies
_____	☐ Relatives	☐ Technology	☐ Music
	☐ Traveling	☐ Nakedness	☐ Work

Date: _____ ☐ ☐ ☐ ☐ ☐ ☐ ☐
Sun Mon Tue Wed Thur Fri Sat

Feelings before sleep: _____

Quality of sleep: ☐ Good   ☐ Medium   ☐ Bad

Type of dream: ☐ Lucid   ☐ Nightmare
                    ☐ Positive   ☐ Other: _____

Have you had these dreams before?

                    ☐ Yes   ☐ No
                    ☐ Multiple   ☐ I don't know

Dream description: _____
_____
_____
_____
_____
_____
_____
_____

Dream interpretation:_____
_____
_____
_____
_____

Time period of the dream: ☐ Past   ☐ Present

                           ☐ Future   ☐ Unknown

Feelings present in the dream:

☐ Fear   ☐ Anger   ☐ Freedom   ☐ Paralysis

☐ Happiness   ☐ Sadness   ☐ Panic   ☐ Love

☐ Doubt   ☐ Boredom   ☐ Peace   ☐ Vulnerability

☐ Luck   ☐ Guilt   ☐ Horror   ☐ Disappointment

☐ Other: _____

The dream featured:

Symbols	Things	Colors	People	Places

Themes	☐ Home	☐ Weather	☐ Fire
☐ Other:	☐ Family	☐ Earth	☐ Water
_____	☐ Childhood	☐ Space	☐ Money
_____	☐ Animals	☐ Vehicles	☐ Health
_____	☐ Friends	☐ Supernatural	☐ Hobbies
_____	☐ Relatives	☐ Technology	☐ Music
	☐ Traveling	☐ Nakedness	☐ Work

Date: _____ ☐ ☐ ☐ ☐ ☐ ☐ ☐
　　　　　　　　　　 Sun　Mon　Tue　Wed　Thur　Fri　Sat

Feelings before sleep: _____

Quality of sleep: ☐ Good ☐ Medium ☐ Bad

Type of dream: ☐ Lucid ☐ Nightmare
　　　　　　　 ☐ Positive ☐ Other: _____

Have you had these dreams before?

☐ Yes ☐ No

☐ Multiple ☐ I don't know

Dream description: _____
_____
_____
_____
_____
_____
_____
_____

Dream interpretation:_____
_____
_____
_____
_____

Time period of the dream: ☐ Past ☐ Present

☐ Future ☐ Unknown

Feelings present in the dream:

☐ Fear ☐ Anger ☐ Freedom ☐ Paralysis

☐ Happiness ☐ Sadness ☐ Panic ☐ Love

☐ Doubt ☐ Boredom ☐ Peace ☐ Vulnerability

☐ Luck ☐ Guilt ☐ Horror ☐ Disappointment

☐ Other: _____

The dream featured:

Symbols	Things	Colors	People	Places

Themes	☐ Home	☐ Weather	☐ Fire
☐ Other:	☐ Family	☐ Earth	☐ Water
_____	☐ Childhood	☐ Space	☐ Money
_____	☐ Animals	☐ Vehicles	☐ Health
_____	☐ Friends	☐ Supernatural	☐ Hobbies
_____	☐ Relatives	☐ Technology	☐ Music
	☐ Traveling	☐ Nakedness	☐ Work

Date: _____ ☐ ☐ ☐ ☐ ☐ ☐ ☐
                        Sun Mon Tue Wed Thur Fri Sat

Feelings before sleep: _____

Quality of sleep: ☐ Good   ☐ Medium   ☐ Bad

Type of dream: ☐ Lucid   ☐ Nightmare
                   ☐ Positive   ☐ Other: _____

Have you had these dreams before?

              ☐ Yes   ☐ No
              ☐ Multiple ☐ I don't know

Dream description: _____
_____
_____
_____
_____
_____
_____
_____

Dream interpretation:_____
_____
_____
_____
_____

Time period of the dream: ☐ Past ☐ Present

☐ Future ☐ Unknown

Feelings present in the dream:

☐ Fear ☐ Anger ☐ Freedom ☐ Paralysis

☐ Happiness ☐ Sadness ☐ Panic ☐ Love

☐ Doubt ☐ Boredom ☐ Peace ☐ Vulnerability

☐ Luck ☐ Guilt ☐ Horror ☐ Disappointment

☐ Other: _____

The dream featured:

Symbols	Things	Colors	People	Places

Themes	☐ Home	☐ Weather	☐ Fire
☐ Other:	☐ Family	☐ Earth	☐ Water
_____	☐ Childhood	☐ Space	☐ Money
_____	☐ Animals	☐ Vehicles	☐ Health
_____	☐ Friends	☐ Supernatural	☐ Hobbies
_____	☐ Relatives	☐ Technology	☐ Music
	☐ Traveling	☐ Nakedness	☐ Work

Date: _____ ☐ ☐ ☐ ☐ ☐ ☐ ☐
Sun   Mon   Tue   Wed   Thur   Fri   Sat

Feelings before sleep: _____

Quality of sleep: ☐ Good   ☐ Medium   ☐ Bad

Type of dream: ☐ Lucid   ☐ Nightmare
                 ☐ Positive   ☐ Other: _____

Have you had these dreams before?

☐ Yes   ☐ No
☐ Multiple ☐ I don't know

Dream description: _____
_____
_____
_____
_____
_____
_____
_____

Dream interpretation:_____
_____
_____
_____
_____

Time period of the dream: ☐ Past ☐ Present

☐ Future ☐ Unknown

Feelings present in the dream:

☐ Fear ☐ Anger ☐ Freedom ☐ Paralysis

☐ Happiness ☐ Sadness ☐ Panic ☐ Love

☐ Doubt ☐ Boredom ☐ Peace ☐ Vulnerability

☐ Luck ☐ Guilt ☐ Horror ☐ Disappointment

☐ Other: _____

The dream featured:

Symbols	Things	Colors	People	Places

Themes	☐ Home	☐ Weather	☐ Fire
☐ Other:	☐ Family	☐ Earth	☐ Water
_____	☐ Childhood	☐ Space	☐ Money
_____	☐ Animals	☐ Vehicles	☐ Health
_____	☐ Friends	☐ Supernatural	☐ Hobbies
_____	☐ Relatives	☐ Technology	☐ Music
	☐ Traveling	☐ Nakedness	☐ Work

Date: _____ ☐   ☐   ☐   ☐   ☐   ☐   ☐
                                     Sun   Mon   Tue   Wed   Thur   Fri   Sat

Feelings before sleep: _____

Quality of sleep: ☐ Good   ☐ Medium   ☐ Bad

Type of dream: ☐ Lucid   ☐ Nightmare
                        ☐ Positive   ☐ Other: _____

Have you had these dreams before?

                ☐ Yes   ☐ No
                ☐ Multiple   ☐ I don't know

Dream description: _____

_____

_____

_____

_____

_____

_____

_____

Dream interpretation:_____

_____

_____

_____

_____

Time period of the dream: ☐ Past ☐ Present

☐ Future ☐ Unknown

Feelings present in the dream:

☐ Fear ☐ Anger ☐ Freedom ☐ Paralysis

☐ Happiness ☐ Sadness ☐ Panic ☐ Love

☐ Doubt ☐ Boredom ☐ Peace ☐ Vulnerability

☐ Luck ☐ Guilt ☐ Horror ☐ Disappointment

☐ Other: _____

The dream featured:

Symbols	Things	Colors	People	Places

Themes	☐ Home	☐ Weather	☐ Fire
☐ Other:	☐ Family	☐ Earth	☐ Water
_____	☐ Childhood	☐ Space	☐ Money
_____	☐ Animals	☐ Vehicles	☐ Health
_____	☐ Friends	☐ Supernatural	☐ Hobbies
_____	☐ Relatives	☐ Technology	☐ Music
	☐ Traveling	☐ Nakedness	☐ Work

Date: _____ ☐ ☐ ☐ ☐ ☐ ☐ ☐
                     Sun Mon Tue Wed Thur Fri Sat

Feelings before sleep: _____

Quality of sleep: ☐ Good   ☐ Medium   ☐ Bad

Type of dream: ☐ Lucid   ☐ Nightmare
                     ☐ Positive ☐ Other: _____

Have you had these dreams before?

                     ☐ Yes   ☐ No
                     ☐ Multiple   ☐ I don't know

Dream description: _____
_____
_____
_____
_____
_____
_____

Dream interpretation:_____
_____
_____
_____
_____

Time period of the dream: ☐ Past   ☐ Present

☐ Future   ☐ Unknown

Feelings present in the dream:

☐ Fear   ☐ Anger   ☐ Freedom   ☐ Paralysis

☐ Happiness   ☐ Sadness   ☐ Panic   ☐ Love

☐ Doubt   ☐ Boredom   ☐ Peace   ☐ Vulnerability

☐ Luck   ☐ Guilt   ☐ Horror   ☐ Disappointment

☐ Other: _____

The dream featured:

Symbols	Things	Colors	People	Places

Themes	☐ Home	☐ Weather	☐ Fire
☐ Other:	☐ Family	☐ Earth	☐ Water
_____	☐ Childhood	☐ Space	☐ Money
_____	☐ Animals	☐ Vehicles	☐ Health
_____	☐ Friends	☐ Supernatural	☐ Hobbies
_____	☐ Relatives	☐ Technology	☐ Music
	☐ Traveling	☐ Nakedness	☐ Work

Date: _____ ☐ ☐ ☐ ☐ ☐ ☐ ☐
                             Sun Mon Tue Wed Thur Fri Sat

Feelings before sleep: _____

Quality of sleep: ☐ Good ☐ Medium ☐ Bad

Type of dream: ☐ Lucid ☐ Nightmare
                       ☐ Positive ☐ Other: _____

Have you had these dreams before?

            ☐ Yes   ☐ No
            ☐ Multiple ☐ I don't know

Dream description: _____
_____
_____
_____
_____
_____
_____

Dream interpretation: _____
_____
_____
_____
_____

Time period of the dream: ☐ Past   ☐ Present

☐ Future   ☐ Unknown

Feelings present in the dream:

☐ Fear   ☐ Anger   ☐ Freedom   ☐ Paralysis

☐ Happiness   ☐ Sadness   ☐ Panic   ☐ Love

☐ Doubt   ☐ Boredom   ☐ Peace   ☐ Vulnerability

☐ Luck   ☐ Guilt   ☐ Horror   ☐ Disappointment

☐ Other: _____

The dream featured:

Symbols	Things	Colors	People	Places

Themes	☐ Home	☐ Weather	☐ Fire
☐ Other:	☐ Family	☐ Earth	☐ Water
_____	☐ Childhood	☐ Space	☐ Money
_____	☐ Animals	☐ Vehicles	☐ Health
_____	☐ Friends	☐ Supernatural	☐ Hobbies
_____	☐ Relatives	☐ Technology	☐ Music
_____	☐ Traveling	☐ Nakedness	☐ Work

Date: _____ ☐ ☐ ☐ ☐ ☐ ☐ ☐
Sun   Mon   Tue   Wed   Thur   Fri   Sat

Feelings before sleep: _____

Quality of sleep: ☐ Good   ☐ Medium   ☐ Bad

Type of dream: ☐ Lucid   ☐ Nightmare
                 ☐ Positive   ☐ Other: _____

Have you had these dreams before?

☐ Yes   ☐ No
☐ Multiple ☐ I don't know

Dream description: _____
_____
_____
_____
_____
_____
_____
_____

Dream interpretation:_____
_____
_____
_____
_____

Time period of the dream:

☐ Past ☐ Present

☐ Future ☐ Unknown

Feelings present in the dream:

☐ Fear ☐ Anger ☐ Freedom ☐ Paralysis

☐ Happiness ☐ Sadness ☐ Panic ☐ Love

☐ Doubt ☐ Boredom ☐ Peace ☐ Vulnerability

☐ Luck ☐ Guilt ☐ Horror ☐ Disappointment

☐ Other: _____

The dream featured:

Symbols	Things	Colors	People	Places

Themes	☐ Home	☐ Weather	☐ Fire
☐ Other:	☐ Family	☐ Earth	☐ Water
_____	☐ Childhood	☐ Space	☐ Money
_____	☐ Animals	☐ Vehicles	☐ Health
_____	☐ Friends	☐ Supernatural	☐ Hobbies
_____	☐ Relatives	☐ Technology	☐ Music
	☐ Traveling	☐ Nakedness	☐ Work

Date: _____ ☐ ☐ ☐ ☐ ☐ ☐ ☐
Sun Mon Tue Wed Thur Fri Sat

Feelings before sleep: _____

Quality of sleep: ☐ Good   ☐ Medium ☐ Bad

Type of dream: ☐ Lucid   ☐ Nightmare
☐ Positive   ☐ Other: _____

Have you had these dreams before?

☐ Yes   ☐ No
☐ Multiple ☐ I don't know

Dream description: _____
_____
_____
_____
_____
_____
_____

Dream interpretation: _____
_____
_____
_____
_____

Time period of the dream: ☐ Past ☐ Present

☐ Future ☐ Unknown

Feelings present in the dream:

☐ Fear ☐ Anger ☐ Freedom ☐ Paralysis

☐ Happiness ☐ Sadness ☐ Panic ☐ Love

☐ Doubt ☐ Boredom ☐ Peace ☐ Vulnerability

☐ Luck ☐ Guilt ☐ Horror ☐ Disappointment

☐ Other: _____

The dream featured:

Symbols	Things	Colors	People	Places

Themes	☐ Home	☐ Weather	☐ Fire
☐ Other:	☐ Family	☐ Earth	☐ Water
_____	☐ Childhood	☐ Space	☐ Money
_____	☐ Animals	☐ Vehicles	☐ Health
_____	☐ Friends	☐ Supernatural	☐ Hobbies
_____	☐ Relatives	☐ Technology	☐ Music
_____	☐ Traveling	☐ Nakedness	☐ Work

Date: _____ ☐ ☐ ☐ ☐ ☐ ☐ ☐
Sun   Mon   Tue   Wed   Thur   Fri   Sat

Feelings before sleep: _____

Quality of sleep: ☐ Good   ☐ Medium   ☐ Bad

Type of dream: ☐ Lucid   ☐ Nightmare
                ☐ Positive   ☐ Other: _____

Have you had these dreams before?

        ☐ Yes   ☐ No
        ☐ Multiple ☐ I don't know

Dream description: _____
_____
_____
_____
_____
_____
_____
_____

Dream interpretation:_____
_____
_____
_____
_____

Time period of the dream: ☐ Past ☐ Present

☐ Future ☐ Unknown

Feelings present in the dream:

☐ Fear ☐ Anger ☐ Freedom ☐ Paralysis

☐ Happiness ☐ Sadness ☐ Panic ☐ Love

☐ Doubt ☐ Boredom ☐ Peace ☐ Vulnerability

☐ Luck ☐ Guilt ☐ Horror ☐ Disappointment

☐ Other: _____

The dream featured:

Symbols	Things	Colors	People	Places

Themes	
☐ Other:	☐ Home ☐ Weather ☐ Fire
_____	☐ Family ☐ Earth ☐ Water
_____	☐ Childhood ☐ Space ☐ Money
_____	☐ Animals ☐ Vehicles ☐ Health
_____	☐ Friends ☐ Supernatural ☐ Hobbies
_____	☐ Relatives ☐ Technology ☐ Music
	☐ Traveling ☐ Nakedness ☐ Work

Date: _____ ☐   ☐   ☐   ☐   ☐   ☐   ☐
                      Sun   Mon   Tue   Wed   Thur   Fri   Sat

Feelings before sleep: _____

Quality of sleep: ☐ Good   ☐ Medium   ☐ Bad

Type of dream: ☐ Lucid   ☐ Nightmare
                        ☐ Positive   ☐ Other: _____

Have you had these dreams before?

                ☐ Yes   ☐ No

                ☐ Multiple   ☐ I don't know

Dream description: _____

_____

_____

_____

_____

_____

_____

_____

Dream interpretation:_____

_____

_____

_____

_____

Time period of the dream: ☐ Past ☐ Present

☐ Future ☐ Unknown

Feelings present in the dream:

☐ Fear ☐ Anger ☐ Freedom ☐ Paralysis

☐ Happiness ☐ Sadness ☐ Panic ☐ Love

☐ Doubt ☐ Boredom ☐ Peace ☐ Vulnerability

☐ Luck ☐ Guilt ☐ Horror ☐ Disappointment

☐ Other: _____

The dream featured:

Symbols	Things	Colors	People	Places

Themes	☐ Home	☐ Weather	☐ Fire
☐ Other:	☐ Family	☐ Earth	☐ Water
_____	☐ Childhood	☐ Space	☐ Money
_____	☐ Animals	☐ Vehicles	☐ Health
_____	☐ Friends	☐ Supernatural	☐ Hobbies
_____	☐ Relatives	☐ Technology	☐ Music
	☐ Traveling	☐ Nakedness	☐ Work

Date: _____ ☐ ☐ ☐ ☐ ☐ ☐ ☐
                          Sun Mon Tue Wed Thur Fri Sat

Feelings before sleep: _____

Quality of sleep: ☐ Good   ☐ Medium ☐ Bad

Type of dream: ☐ Lucid   ☐ Nightmare
                        ☐ Positive ☐ Other: _____

Have you had these dreams before?

                  ☐ Yes   ☐ No
                  ☐ Multiple ☐ I don't know

Dream description: _____
_____
_____
_____
_____
_____
_____

Dream interpretation: _____
_____
_____
_____
_____

Time period of the dream: ☐ Past ☐ Present

☐ Future ☐ Unknown

Feelings present in the dream:

☐ Fear ☐ Anger ☐ Freedom ☐ Paralysis

☐ Happiness ☐ Sadness ☐ Panic ☐ Love

☐ Doubt ☐ Boredom ☐ Peace ☐ Vulnerability

☐ Luck ☐ Guilt ☐ Horror ☐ Disappointment

☐ Other: _____

The dream featured:

Symbols	Things	Colors	People	Places

Themes	☐ Home	☐ Weather	☐ Fire
☐ Other:	☐ Family	☐ Earth	☐ Water
_____	☐ Childhood	☐ Space	☐ Money
_____	☐ Animals	☐ Vehicles	☐ Health
_____	☐ Friends	☐ Supernatural	☐ Hobbies
_____	☐ Relatives	☐ Technology	☐ Music
	☐ Traveling	☐ Nakedness	☐ Work

Date: _____ ☐ ☐ ☐ ☐ ☐ ☐ ☐
　　　　　　　　　　　　Sun　Mon　Tue　Wed　Thur　Fri　Sat

Feelings before sleep: _____

Quality of sleep:　　☐ Good　　☐ Medium　☐ Bad

Type of dream:　　　☐ Lucid　　☐ Nightmare
　　　　　　　　　　☐ Positive　☐ Other: _____

Have you had these dreams before?

　　　　　　　☐ Yes　　☐ No
　　　　　　　☐ Multiple　☐ I don't know

Dream description: _____
_____
_____
_____
_____
_____
_____
_____

Dream interpretation: _____
_____
_____
_____
_____

Time period of the dream: ☐ Past   ☐ Present

                                         ☐ Future   ☐ Unknown

Feelings present in the dream:

☐ Fear   ☐ Anger   ☐ Freedom   ☐ Paralysis

☐ Happiness   ☐ Sadness   ☐ Panic   ☐ Love

☐ Doubt   ☐ Boredom   ☐ Peace   ☐ Vulnerability

☐ Luck   ☐ Guilt   ☐ Horror   ☐ Disappointment

☐ Other: _____

The dream featured:

Symbols	Things	Colors	People	Places

Themes	☐ Home	☐ Weather	☐ Fire
☐ Other:	☐ Family	☐ Earth	☐ Water
_____	☐ Childhood	☐ Space	☐ Money
_____	☐ Animals	☐ Vehicles	☐ Health
_____	☐ Friends	☐ Supernatural	☐ Hobbies
_____	☐ Relatives	☐ Technology	☐ Music
	☐ Traveling	☐ Nakedness	☐ Work

Date: _____ ☐   ☐   ☐   ☐   ☐   ☐   ☐
                              Sun   Mon   Tue   Wed   Thur   Fri   Sat

Feelings before sleep: _____

Quality of sleep: ☐ Good   ☐ Medium   ☐ Bad

Type of dream: ☐ Lucid   ☐ Nightmare
                     ☐ Positive   ☐ Other: _____

Have you had these dreams before?

            ☐ Yes   ☐ No
            ☐ Multiple ☐ I don't know

Dream description: _____

_____

_____

_____

_____

_____

_____

Dream interpretation:_____

_____

_____

_____

_____

Time period of the dream: ☐ Past   ☐ Present

☐ Future   ☐ Unknown

Feelings present in the dream:

☐ Fear ☐ Anger ☐ Freedom ☐ Paralysis

☐ Happiness ☐ Sadness ☐ Panic ☐ Love

☐ Doubt ☐ Boredom ☐ Peace ☐ Vulnerability

☐ Luck ☐ Guilt ☐ Horror ☐ Disappointment

☐ Other: _____

The dream featured:

Symbols	Things	Colors	People	Places

Themes	☐ Home	☐ Weather	☐ Fire
☐ Other:	☐ Family	☐ Earth	☐ Water
_____	☐ Childhood	☐ Space	☐ Money
_____	☐ Animals	☐ Vehicles	☐ Health
_____	☐ Friends	☐ Supernatural	☐ Hobbies
_____	☐ Relatives	☐ Technology	☐ Music
_____	☐ Traveling	☐ Nakedness	☐ Work

Date: _____ ☐ ☐ ☐ ☐ ☐ ☐ ☐
　　　　　　　　　 Sun　Mon　Tue　Wed　Thur　Fri　Sat

Feelings before sleep: _____

Quality of sleep: ☐ Good ☐ Medium ☐ Bad

Type of dream: ☐ Lucid ☐ Nightmare
　　　　　　　 ☐ Positive ☐ Other: _____

Have you had these dreams before?

☐ Yes ☐ No

☐ Multiple ☐ I don't know

Dream description: _____
_____
_____
_____
_____
_____
_____

Dream interpretation:_____
_____
_____
_____
_____

Time period of the dream: ☐ Past ☐ Present

☐ Future ☐ Unknown

Feelings present in the dream:

☐ Fear ☐ Anger ☐ Freedom ☐ Paralysis

☐ Happiness ☐ Sadness ☐ Panic ☐ Love

☐ Doubt ☐ Boredom ☐ Peace ☐ Vulnerability

☐ Luck ☐ Guilt ☐ Horror ☐ Disappointment

☐ Other: _____

The dream featured:

Symbols	Things	Colors	People	Places

Themes	☐ Home	☐ Weather	☐ Fire
☐ Other:	☐ Family	☐ Earth	☐ Water
_____	☐ Childhood	☐ Space	☐ Money
_____	☐ Animals	☐ Vehicles	☐ Health
_____	☐ Friends	☐ Supernatural	☐ Hobbies
_____	☐ Relatives	☐ Technology	☐ Music
_____	☐ Traveling	☐ Nakedness	☐ Work